BEST OF

Hong Kong

Steve Fallon

Best of Hong Kong
3rd edition – April 2005
First published – January 2001

Published by Lonely Planet Publications Pty Ltd
ABN 36 005 607 983

Australia	Head Office, Locked Bag 1, Footscray, Vic 3011
	☎ 03 8379 8000 fax 03 8379 8111
	🖳 talk2us@lonelyplanet.com.au
USA	150 Linden St, Oakland, CA 94607
	☎ 510 893 8555 toll free 800 275 8555
	fax 510 893 8572
	🖳 info@lonelyplanet.com
UK	72–82 Rosebery Avenue, London EC1R 4RW
	☎ 020 7841 9000 fax 020 7841 9001
	🖳 go@lonelyplanet.co.uk

This title was commissioned in Lonely Planet's Melbourne office and produced by: **Commissioning Editor** Rebecca Chau **Coordinating Editor** Katrina Webb **Coordinating Cartographer** Kusnandar **Cartographer** Jenny Jones **Layout Designer** Mik Ruff **Editor** Craig Kilburn **Indexer** Katrina Webb **Managing Cartographer** Corinne Waddell **Series Designer** Brendan Dempsey **Cover Designer** Julie Rovis **Cover Artwork** Wendy Wright **Project Manager** Eoin Dunlevy **Mapping Development** Paul Piaia **Regional Publishing Manager** Kate Cody **Thanks to** Adriana Mammarella, Kate MacDonald, Sally Darmody, Mark Germanchis, Bruce Evans, Ryan Evans, Glenn Beanland, Fiona Siseman, Celia Wood, Lachlan Ross, Jacqueline McLeod

Photographs by Lonely Planet Images and Phil Weymouth except for the following: p64, p67, p84 Frank Carter/Lonely Planet Images, p43 Lee Foster/Lonely Planet Images, p92 Rick Gerharter/Lonely Planet Images, p34, p90, p99 John Hay/Lonely Planet Images, p22, p47, p48, p52 Richard l'Anson/Lonely Planet Images, p68 Oliver Strewe/Lonely Planet Images, p91 Dallas Stribley/Lonely Planet Images, p83 Michael Taylor/Lonely Planet Images, p37 Julia Wilkinson/Lonely Planet Images. **Cover photograph** Neon lights and streets of Kowloon, Glen Allison/Getty Images. All images are copyright of the photographers unless otherwise indicated. Many of the images in this guide are available for licensing from Lonely Planet Images: 🖳 www.lonelyplanetimages.com

ISBN 174059844X

Printed by Markono Print Media Pte Ltd, Singapore

HOW TO USE THIS BOOK

Colour-Coding & Maps

Each chapter has a colour code along the banner at the top of the page which is also used for text and symbols on maps (eg all venues reviewed in the Highlights chapter are orange on the maps). The fold-out maps inside the front and back covers are numbered from 1 to 7. All sights and venues in the text have map references; eg (3, B5) means Map 3, grid reference B5. See p128 for map symbols.

Prices

Multiple prices listed with reviews (eg $10/5) usually indicate adult/concession admission to a venue. Concession prices can include senior, student, member or coupon discounts. Meal cost and room rate categories are listed at the start of the Eating and Sleeping chapters, respectively.

Text Symbols

☎	telephone
✉	address
🖳	email/website address
$	admission
☽	opening hours
ⓘ	information
🚌	bus
⚓	ferry
Ⓜ	metro
🚆	train
🚋	tram
Ⓟ	parking available
♿	wheelchair access
✗	on site/nearby eatery
♣	child-friendly venue
Ⓥ	good vegetarian selection

Contents

From the Publisher

AUTHOR

Steve Fallon

A native of Boston, Massachusetts, Steve graduated from Georgetown University with a Bachelor of Science in modern languages, including Chinese. After he had worked for several years for an American daily newspaper and earned a master's degree in journalism, Steve's fascination with the 'new' Asia took him to Hong Kong, where he lived for over 12 years working for a variety of media and running a travel bookshop. He has contributed to or written more than two dozen Lonely Planet titles, including *Hong Kong & Macau* and *China*.

In Hong Kong, thanks to Rocky Dang of Phoenix Services Agency, Margaret Leung of Get Smart and Rob Stewart of Bloomberg for their generous assistance. I'm also grateful to Teresa Costa Gomes of the Macau Government Tourist Office for her help and support.

The 1st edition of this book was written by Dani Valent. The 2nd edition was written by Patrick Witton.

PHOTOGRAPHER

Phil Weymouth

Phil's family moved from Australia to Iran in the late 1960s and called Tehran home until the revolution in 1979. Phil studied photography in Melbourne and returned to the Middle East to work as a photographer in Bahrain for several years. He then spent a decade working with an Australian rural media company. Currently he runs a freelance photojournalism business based in Melbourne, working for a variety of Australian and international media and publishing companies.

Past commissions for Lonely Planet include the guides to *Hong Kong, Beijing, Shanghai, Istanbul, Singapore* and *Dubai*. Phil continues to travel extensively, supplying images to Lonely Planet Images, writing stories and avoiding his office.

Introducing Hong Kong

Hong Kong is a million different things to a million different people. You might be shopping for 1000-year-old eggs and pungent durian fruit at a tatty market stall in the shadow of a gleaming skyscraper when your mobile phone rings. Or perhaps you're snacking on chicken's feet next to a woman who's sporting a Louis Vuitton bag and wearing a Hello Kitty hairclip and T-shirt that says 'Some Things Un-understandable'. Or maybe you're heading back to your room after celebrating the closing of a deal at a seafood restaurant with prime harbour views when the concierge glides up to say your suit is ready for the second fitting.

Hong Kong has all the usual big-city blues – pollution, 14 million elbows and an insane love of clatter – but it's also efficient, peaceful and surprisingly green. The transport network is excellent, the shopping centres are sublime and the temples and parks are contemplative oases.

It's an intoxicating place; spectacular, exotic and accessible. The food is fantastic, there are some great hotels, doing business is a breeze and there's a surprising range of nature-loving getaways within easy reach.

Hong Kong is a pulsating, superlative-ridden fusion of West and East, an exercise in controlled chaos, and a densely populated place that simply 'shouldn't be, but is'. It's like no other city on earth.

The view from the famous glass curtain of the Hong Kong Convention & Exhibition Centre

Districts & Islands

Hong Kong is made up of four main areas: Hong Kong Island (80 sq km) to the south; the Kowloon peninsula (47 sq km) across the harbour to the north; the New Territories (798 sq km), which sprawl northward from Kowloon to mainland China; and the 234 Outlying Islands (177 sq km).

HONG KONG ISLAND (2)

Though it makes up just over 7% of the territory's land area, the island is home to most of the major businesses and government offices and many top-end hotels and restaurants.

Every visitor to Hong Kong makes it to **Central** on the island's northern shore, be it for sightseeing, business, transport (eg the Outlying Islands are most conveniently reached from Central) or entertainment in the Lan Kwai Fong or Soho nightlife districts; see p40 for a Central amble. Bordering Central to the west is **Sheung Wan**, parts of which have retained the feel of pre-war Hong Kong – you'll find a walking tour on p41. Rising above the two districts is the residential area of the **Mid-Levels** and **Victoria Peak** (p10).

Just east of Central, **Admiralty** is essentially a clump of office towers, hotels and shopping malls, including the excellent Pacific Place. Contiguous with Admiralty is **Wan Chai**, a seedy red-light district during the Vietnam War but now a popular entertainment spot, with bars and clubs lining Jaffe and Lockhart Rds.

Further east, frantic **Causeway Bay** is the most popular shopping area on the island. People also visit the district to eat and, to a lesser extent, pub-crawl.

The more tranquil south side of Hong Kong Island is made up of (east to west): **Shek O**, which is now something of an activities centre; **Stanley**, with its fashionable restaurants and famous market; posh **Repulse Bay**, where you'll find one of the most popular beaches on the island; and **Aberdeen**, where you can ride in a sampan or a junk around the harbour (p49), eat at a floating restaurant (p75), or visit the nearby Ocean Park amusement and theme park (p39).

KOWLOON (3)

Kowloon (Nine Dragons), which stretches northwards from the harbour, officially ends in Mong Kok, but the area's malls and glittering hotels continue to spread northward into what is now called New Kowloon.

It's a bird, a skate, a lotus petal, a banana leaf...?

Located at the southern end of the peninsula, **Tsim Sha Tsui** (pronounced 'jim sa joy') is Hong Kong's tourist ghetto, with countless clothing and electronics shops, hotels, restaurants and sleazy bars crammed into a tiny area. **Tsim Sha Tsui East**, the triangular block of reclaimed land east of Chatham Rd South, is a cluster of shopping malls, nightclubs, top-end hotels and two world-class museums.

Puffing to the top of one of Lantau's most visited attractions

Just north of 'Tsimsy' is **Yau Ma Tei** (pronounced 'yow ma day'), whose narrow streets are good places to check out Hong Kong's more traditional urban society. Within the square bordered by Kansu St, Nanking St, Woo Sung St and Canton Rd, you'll come across pawnshops, Chinese pharmacies, mah jong parlours and the Temple St Night Market (p16).

Mong Kok is Hong Kong's most congested working-class residential areas, as well as one of its busiest shopping districts, especially for clothing, household goods and computers. In the streets west of Nathan Rd are some of the city's seedier brothels. See p42 for a self-guided walk around the area.

NEW TERRITORIES & ISLANDS (1)

The New Territories, once Hong Kong's country playground, is today a mixed bag of congested 'New Towns' such as **Tsuen Wan** and **Sha Tin** and some surprisingly unspoiled rural areas and country parks like **Sai Kung East Country Park** (p46) and the protected **Mai Po Marsh**.

Most of Hong Kong's islands are uninhabited and/or inaccessible, but those that can be reached by public ferry include: **Cheung Chau** (p43), with its traditional village and fishing fleet; **Lamma** (p46), famed for its restaurants; and **Lantau** (p44), with its excellent beaches and trails.

Off the Beaten Track
It *is* possible to get away from it all in manic Hong Kong, and the following lesser-known attractions are good spots to chill out:
- Chi Lin Nunnery (p36)
- Hong Kong Heritage Museum (p26)
- Kowloon Walled City Park (p34)
- Lei Cheng Uk Han Tomb Museum (p28)
- Ten Thousand Buddhas Monastery (p22)
- Lam Tsuen Wishing Tree (p37)
- Tin Hau Temple (p37)

Itineraries

Hong Kong is awash with things to see and do – from world-class museums and markets as rich as Aladdin's Cave to harbour boat rides and breathtaking country walks. If your time is limited, take an organised tour (p49) or follow any of the itineraries below.

DAY ONE
Catch the tram up to the Peak (p10) for an overview of the city. Stretch your legs on a summit circuit before lunching at the Peak Lookout. Return to Central and tram to Sheung Wan for souvenir shopping at Western Market (p35) and along Cat St. Spend the evening in Lan Kwai Fong.

DAY TWO
Take the Star Ferry (p9) to Tsim Sha Tsui and visit the Hong Kong Museum of History (p13) or Museum of Art (p26). Have dim sum at Wan Loong Court then browse along Nathan Rd until you're ready for tea at the Peninsula Hong Kong hotel (p19). End the day with a wander up Temple St (p16) through the night market.

DAY THREE
Explore Central's shops and galleries before lunching in Soho (p69). Take a tram to Wan Chai for a night of high-brow classical entertainment at the Hong Kong Arts Centre (p91). Strut your stuff at a Wan Chai club before dining late at 369 Shanghai (p72).

Lowlights
Hong Kong is not without its downsides.
- Noise pollution – when will they finish building and why won't taxi drivers turn down the Cantopop?
- Crowds – they're everywhere at all times and always directly in your path.
- Air pollution – could there be more cars and trucks than trees here?
- Air conditioners – they turn buses into fridges on wheels and drip on passers-by from high-rise blocks.
- Expensive booze – OK, tax on beer is 40% but must a pint cost as much as $50?
- Rudeness – less of a problem than in the past, but all of the above can contribute to a certain amount of irritability and impatience.

Still thinking about hiring a car to get around...?

Highlights

STAR FERRY (3, B9)

Since 1888, oval-shaped double-decker ferries have chugged back and forth between Kowloon (4, B3) and Hong Kong Island. Over the decades

INFORMATION

- ☎ 2367 7065
- 🖳 www.starferry .com.hk
- $ upper/lower deck adult $2.20/1.30, child $1.70/1.30, 65 & over free
- ⏱ 6.30am-11.30pm
- ♿ fair (on the lower deck only)
- ✖ Maxim's Palace (boxed text p66)

land reclamation (see the boxed text p12) has made the journey shorter, while rampant development has turned it into one of the most spectacular commutes anywhere. Morning and evening, the *Star Ferry* is a common way for local people to hop from island to mainland and back again. Indeed, until the Cross-Harbour Tunnel opened in 1978 and the first line of the Mass Transit Railway (MTR; p112) two years later, the *Star Ferry* was the *only* way to cross the harbour. At rush hour long queues of commuters would back up as far as the General Post Office on the Hong Kong side and Star House in Kowloon.

With names like *Morning Star, Night Star, Celestial Star* and *Twinkling Star*, the ferries are most romantic at night. The boats are festively strung with lights, the city buildings beam onto the rippling water, the frenzy of Hong Kong by day has eased (somewhat) and canoodling appears the only sensible thing to do.

There are four cross-harbour *Star Ferry* routes, but by far the most popular is the seven-minute run between Tsim Sha Tsui and Central (in that direction – it's not half as dramatic from Hong Kong Island to Kowloon). Boats depart every four to 10 minutes.

Trouble Afloat

There are few modes of transport that can claim they sparked a riot, but the *Star Ferry* can. In 1966, when China was locked in the grip of the fiasco they now call the Cultural Revolution, Hong Kong–based Communist agitators used the ferry company's fare increase of 5c as pretext for fomenting violent demonstrations. The disturbances continued for almost a year.

VICTORIA PEAK (2, A2)

On your first clear day, get your booty up here; if you haven't been to the Peak, then you haven't been to Hong Kong. Not only is the view from the summit one of the most spectacular cityscapes in the world, it's also a good way to get Hong Kong into perspective. Repeat the trip up on a clear night too as the illuminated outlook is superb.

INFORMATION

- ☎ 2849 7654, 2849 0668
- 🖳 www.thepeak .com.hk
- ✉ 33 Garden Rd, Central/128 Peak Rd (Peak Tram lower/upper terminus)
- 🚌 15 (from Exchange Square), minibus 1 (from City Hall)
- ♿ good (not on the Peak Tram)
- ✗ Peak Lookout (p72), Cafe Deco (p71), Mövenpick Marché (p71)

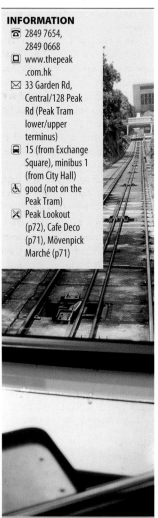

Brave the Peak Tram for views meant for the gods

The Peak has been *the* place to live ever since the British arrived. The taipans built summer houses here to escape the heat and humidity (it's usually about 5°C cooler than down below). The Peak remains the most fashionable – and expensive – area to live in Hong Kong.

When people here refer to the Peak, they generally mean the plateau and surrounding residential area at about 400m. The summit, Victoria Peak (552m), is about 500m northwest of the Peak Tram terminus up steep Mt Austin Rd. The **governor's mountain lodge** near the summit was burned to the ground by the Japanese during WWII, but the **gardens** remain and are open to the public.

You can walk around Victoria Peak without exhausting yourself. Harlech Rd on the south side and Lugard Rd on the northern slope together form a 3.5km loop that takes about an hour to walk. If you feel like a longer walk, you can continue for a further 2km along Peak Rd to Pok Fu Lam Reservoir

The Way Up There

'Removed high above the dust and noise of the town, the Peak Hotel offers the traveller those few days of quiet rest so necessary after a long sea voyage. Rates per day from $5.00 up.'
Hongkong and its Vicinity, 1911

Rd, which leaves Peak Rd near the car park exit. This goes past the reservoir to the main Pok Fu Lam Rd, where you can get the No 7 bus to Aberdeen or back to Central.

Another good walk leads down to **Hong Kong University** (2, A2). First walk to the west side of Victoria Peak by taking either Lugard or Harlech Rds. After reaching Hatton Rd, follow it down.

Rising above the Peak Tram terminus is the seven-storey **Peak Tower** (4, A6), an anvil-shaped building containing shops, restaurants and several attractions suitable for kids and open from 10am to 10pm daily. Choose among the **Peak Explorer Motion Simulator** ($62/35), a futuristic ride in space, on the 4th level; **Ripley's Believe it or Not! Odditorium** ($90/50) on the 3rd level; and an outpost of **Madame Tussaud's** ($95/55) on the 2nd level. The kid-friendly restaurant **Mövenpick Marché** (p71) is on levels 6 and 7, and there is a **viewing terrace** with coin-operated binoculars on level 5.

You should catch the **Peak Tram** (p113) at least one way. It's such a steep ride that the floor is angled to help standing passengers stay upright. In 1885 everyone thought that Phineas Kyrie and William Kerfoot Hughes were crazy when they announced their intention to build a funicular to the top of the peak, but it opened successfully three years later, wiping out the sedan-chair trade overnight. Since then, the tram has never had an accident (a comforting thought if you start to have doubts about the strength of the cable), and has been stopped only by WWII, and the violent rainstorms of 1966 which washed half the track down the hillside.

> **DON'T MISS**
> - Riding the Peak Tram from the top down
> - Finding your hotel on the skyline from the viewing deck
> - Walking to the Peak summit

East meets West: Hong Kong's striking skyline of corporate towers

TSIM SHA TSUI PROMENADE (3, B9)

Stretching along what is arguably the most dramatic harbour in the world, this open-air walkway offers superb views of Hong Kong Island. The best time to take a promenade perambulation is at night, when the view of Central lit up like a million Chinese lanterns is nothing short of mesmerising and you can happily turn your back on the landfill that is Tsim Sha Tsui East. Some nights half of Hong Kong seems to make its way down to enjoy the view, and you'll find yourself sharing space with joggers, lovers, musicians, families and people fishing right off the walkway. There's also a raised viewing platform near the former **KCR Clock Tower**. You can walk from the *Star Ferry* pier almost all the way to the Hong Kong Coliseum and Hung Hom train station. Toward the end of the promenade is the Tsim Sha Tsui East ferry pier from where you can catch a hydrofoil to Central.

Quite a lengthy stretch of the promenade that runs northeast from in front of the Hotel Inter-Continental is christened **Avenue of the Stars.** It pays homage to the Hong Kong film industry and its stars, with handprints, sculptures and a spectacular light show daily at 8pm.

The view is impressive during the day as well, but the heat and pollution can sap your strength, especially in summer. Luckily the **Hong Kong Museum of Art** (p26), **Hong Kong Space Museum** (p28) and **Teddy Bear Kingdom** (p39) all line the promenade so you can duck in for some shade and a change of scene.

INFORMATION

- ✉ south of Salisbury Rd along Victoria Harbour, Tsim Sha Tsui
- $ free
- 🚢 Star Ferry (Tsim Sha Tsui pier), hydrofoil (Tsim Sha Tsui East pier)
- Ⓜ Tsim Sha Tsui (exit E)
- ♿ excellent
- ✄ Tsim Sha Tsui (p76)

Taking a break from the fast lane

Terra Infirma

Hong Kong isn't what it used to be – it's more. Much of the land covered by the Tsim Sha Tsui promenade and all of Tsim Sha Tsui sits on landfill dumped into Victoria Harbour. In the past two decades, Hong Kong's surface area has grown more than 6% due to this land 'reclamation'.

...ORY (3, D6)

INFORMATION
- ☎ 2724 9042
- 💻 http://hk.history .museum
- ✉ 100 Chatham Rd, Tsim Sha Tsui East
- 💲 $10/5 (free Wed)
- 🕐 10am-6pm Mon & Wed-Sat, 10am-7pm Sun
- ℹ free 90min English-language guided tours at 10.30am & 2.30pm Sat & Sun
- 🚌 5A, 5C, 8 (from Star Ferry Pier)
- Ⓜ Tsim Sha Tsui (exit B2)
- ♿ good
- 🍱 Genki Sushi (p77)

HONG KONG

Commercial...
have its...
ture, bu...
ter sa...
the natu-
...local
...isit, not
...out these
...stand how
...its its past to

...se-built in Tsim Sha ...i East, the Museum of History takes visitors on a fascinating amble through eight galleries that portray the territory's past, starting with the natural environment and prehistoric Hong Kong (around 6000 years ago, give or take a lunar year) and ending with the resumption of Chinese sovereignty in 1997. Along the way you'll encounter replicas of village dwellings, traditional Chinese costumes and beds, and a re-creation of an entire arcaded street in Central from 1881, including an old Chinese medicine shop.

The museum's large collection of 19th- and early 20th-century photographs is fascinating, but a favourite exhibit is still the jumble of toys and collectibles from the 1960s and 1970s when 'Made in Hong Kong' meant 'Christmas stocking trash'.

DON'T MISS
- Multimedia presentations from Stone Age to Cyber Age
- 1913 vintage tram
- Japanese Occupation gallery showing interviews with POWs
- Handover footage set to moving music

The eyes say it all...

TIAN TAN BUDDHA STATUE

Perched 500m up in the western hills of La[...]
Buddhist monastery and temple complex co[...]

INFORMATION

- ☎ 2985 5248
- ✉ Ngong Ping Plateau, Lantau
- 💲 statue/museum free/$28 (free if eating at restaurant)
- 🕐 monastery 9am-6pm, statue & museum 10am-6pm
- 🚌 2 (Mui Wo), 11 (Tung Chung & Tai O), 21 (Tai O) & 23 (Tung Chung)
- ✗ vegetarian restaurant on site

...dha stat[...]
tion of the [...]
is some 26.4[...]
34m if you i[...]
There are bigge[...]
elsewhere...but a[...]
are not seated, out[...]
of bronze. The large b[...]
statue is controlled b[...]
and rings 108 times d[...]
day to symbolise escape fro[...]
Buddhism terms the '108 tr[...]
of mankind'.

The podium is composed [...]
separate chambers on three level[...]
and reached by 260 steps. In the
first level are six statues of **Bo-
dhisattvas**, or Buddhist 'saints',
each of which weighs two tonnes.
On the second level is a small
museum containing oil paintings
and ceramic plaques of the Buddha's life and teachings. Entry is
free if you eat at the monastery's
vegetarian restaurant.

The Buddha's Birthday, a public
holiday celebrated in late April or
early May, is a lively time to visit,
when thousands make the pilgrimage. Visitors are requested to ob-
serve some decorum in dress and
behaviour. It is forbidden to bring
meat or alcohol into the grounds.

Prayer and stare: Po Lin's sumptuous interior

DON'T MISS

- Vegetarian set meal (regular/deluxe $60/100)
- Row after row of huge, pollen-yellow incense sticks
- Lantau Peak rising to the southeast
- Lantau Tea Garden, Hong Kong's only tea plantation

HONG KONG TRAMS (4 & 5)

Hong Kong's venerable old trams are the slowest and least flashy way to go, but they're cheap and fun; in fact, apart from the *Star Ferry* (p9),

no form of transport is nearer and dearer to the hearts of most Hong Kong people. These 164 tall, narrow streetcars comprise the world's only fully double-decker tramcar fleet, and they roll (and rock) along the northern coast of Hong Kong Island on 16km of track.

The electric trams began operating in 1904, running from Kennedy Town in the west to Shau Kei Wan in the east. The network has been augmented by five other routes over the decades, all of them passing through Sheung Wan, Central and Admiralty. One route veers off to the southeast to loop around Happy Valley Racecourse (see p24).

When the trams first started running they caused a sensation. Stops were packed with people but not many of them actually wanted to go anywhere; a great number just jumped on, walked through having a gander and treading on toes, then got off again, not quite ready to ride. The trams were also delayed by hawkers who took advantage of the tramway by dragging their heavy carts along the well-made tracks. In 1911, a law was passed banning carts with the same wheel gauge as the trams. The law is still in effect today.

INFORMATION
- ☎ 2548 7102
- 🖥 www.info.gov.hk /td/eng/transport /tram.html
- 💲 $2/1
- 🕐 6am-12.30pm (hrs vary depending on the route)
- 🚃 Sheung Wan, Central, Admiralty, Wan Chai, Causeway Bay

Slow and steady wins the race

Making Tracks Make Sense

The original tram route dating back over 100 years followed what was then the shoreline of Hong Kong Island, which has now been pushed inland by as much as half a kilometre through land reclamation. This helps to understand why roads curve and dogleg in ways that don't seem quite right.

TEMPLE ST NIGHT MARKET (3, B4)

Temple St, named after the temple dedicated to Tin Hau (p37) at its centre, hosts the liveliest night market in Hong Kong. It is *the* place to go for cheap clothes, *dai pai dong* (open-air street stall) food, watches, pirated CDs and DVDs, fake labels, footwear, cookware and everyday items. It used to be known as 'Men's St' because the market only sold men's clothing and to distinguish it from the 'Ladies Market' (or 'Women's St') on Tung Choi St to the northeast in Mong Kok. Though there are still a lot of items on sale for men, vendors don't discriminate – anyone's money will do.

The night market extends around Jordan Rd in the south to Man Ming Lane in the north and is divided by Tin Hau Temple. For street food, head to the northern section. You can get anything from a simple bowl

INFORMATION
- ✉ Temple St, Yau Ma Tei
- $ free
- ⊙ 4pm-11pm
- Ⓜ Jordan (exit C2), Yau Ma Tei (exit C)
- ✕ Yau Ma Tei & Mong Kok (p79)

of noodles to a full meal, served at your very own kerbside table. There are a few seafood and hotpot restaurants as well. The market officially opens in the afternoon, but most hawkers set up at about 6pm and are gone by midnight. The market is at its best from about 7pm to 10pm, when it's clogged with stalls and people.

Haggle Gaggle

Any marked prices should be considered mere suggestions – the night market is definitely a place to bargain and bargain hard. To start serious negotiations say *'Peng dak m dak a?'* (Can you reduce the price?). If the stallholder stays high (they'll probably tap the price out on a calculator), say *'Ga chin tai gwai la!'* (That's too expensive!) and see if they budge. Our money says they will.

There's no such thing as a done deal

REPULSE BAY (2, B3)

The long **beach** with tawny sand at Repulse Bay is the most popular on Hong Kong Island. Packed at the weekend and even during the week in summer, it's a good place if you like people-watching.

At the southeastern end of Repulse Bay beach is an unusual shrine to **Kwun Yam**, the God of Mercy. The surrounding area has an amazing assembly of mosaics, deities and figures – goldfish, rams, statues of Tin Hau and other southern Chinese icons. Most of the statues were funded by local personalities and businesspeople during the 1970s.

In front of the Kwun Yam shrine to the left as you face the sea is **Longevity Bridge**; crossing it is supposed to add three days to your life.

Middle Bay and **South Bay**, about 10 minutes and 30 minutes to the south respectively on foot, have beaches that are usually much less crowded than the main beach at Repulse Bay.

Repulse Bay is home to some

INFORMATION
- ⊠ Beach Rd, Repulse Bay
- $ free
- ☺ lifeguards on duty 9am-6pm Mar-May & Sep-Nov, 8am-7pm Jun-Aug
- 🚌 6, 6A, 6X, 260
- ✗ Verandah (p76)

of Hong Kong's richest residents, and the hills around the beach are strewn with luxury apartment blocks, including the pink, blue and yellow wavy number with a giant square hole in the middle called the **Repulse Bay**; apparently this design feature was added on the advice of a feng shui expert. In front of this unusual modern structure stands a **replica** of the wonderful old colonial Repulse Bay Hotel, built in 1922 and razed 60 years later. It contains a small shopping mall and several eateries, including the **Verandah**.

DON'T MISS
- Crossing Longevity Bridge
- Taking tea at the Verandah
- Swimming in South Bay
- Watching couples pose for wedding photos in front of the mock Repulse Bay Hotel

There's just never enough time...

BANK OF CHINA TOWER (4, D4)

Hong Kong's third-tallest structure after **Two IFC** (see the boxed text p31) and **Central Plaza** (7, B4), the 70-storey Bank of China Tower

INFORMATION

- ✉ 1 Garden Rd, Central
- $ free
- ☾ 8am-6pm Mon-Fri
- Ⓜ Central
- 🚇 Admiralty
- ♿ excellent
- ✗ Café (p67), Mix (p68)

Bad Joss Job

Many local people see the tower as a huge violation of the principles of feng shui. For example, the bank's four triangular prisms are negative symbols in the geomancer's rule book; being the opposite to circles, these contradict what circles suggest – perfection and (importantly here) prosperity. Furthermore, the huge crosses on the sides of the building suggest negativity and its shape has been likened to a praying mantis (a threatening symbol), complete with radio masts as antennae.

became something of a symbol of Hong Kong immediately after it was completed in 1990. Impressive and daring as it is, the building is very much a brash and hard-edged synopsis of the 1980s. For 'face' reasons, the tower, representing the People's Republic of China, had to be taller than the nearby Hongkong & Shanghai Bank building (p31), the symbol of the exiting power.

Although it was designed by Chinese-born architect IM Pei, the building is clearly Western in inspiration; 'I didn't design a pagoda' he told journalists when he first unveiled his plans. Chinese elements are incorporated but muted. The segments of the building rising upwards are claimed to be analogous to bamboo sections, and the two-tonne granite base is said to recall Beijing's ancient city gates. The asymmetry of the building is puzzling at first glance, but is really a simple geometric exercise. Rising from the ground like a cube, it is successively reduced, quarter by quarter, until the south-facing side is left to rise upward. The staggered truncation of each triangular column creates a prismatic effect.

Take the express lift to the 43rd floor from where you'll be rewarded with a panoramic view over Hong Kong. From here you are about the same height as the Hongkong and Shanghai Bank to the northwest. It's a pity that you aren't allowed to go any higher, as it's exciting swaying with the wind at the top.

THE PENINSULA (3, C8)

Not just a Hong Kong landmark, the Peninsula Hong Kong is also one of the world's great hotels (p95). Though it was being called 'the finest hotel east of Suez' just a few years after opening in 1928, the Peninsula was in fact one of several prestigious hostelries across Asia where everybody who was anybody stayed, lining up with the likes of Raffles in Singapore, the Peace (then the Cathay) in Shanghai and the Strand in Rangoon (now Yangon).

Land reclamation has robbed the hotel of its top waterfront location, but the breathtaking lobby of the original building is worth a visit and the 20-storey extension offers sweeping views of Hong Kong Island (or Kowloon from your spa).

Taking **afternoon tea** at the Peninsula is one of the best experiences in town – dress neatly and be prepared to queue for a table. While you're waiting, you can listen to the string quartet and salivate at the sight of everyone else's cucumber sandwiches and dainty cakes. From 6pm catch a lift up to **Felix** (p77) on the 28th floor, order a martini and savour the view.

INFORMATION
- ☎ 2920 2888
- 🖳 www.peninsula.com
- ✉ Salisbury Rd, Tsim Sha Tsui
- 💲 afternoon tea $180-220
- 🕒 afternoon tea 2-7pm
- ⚓ Star Ferry
- Ⓜ Tsim Sha Tsui
- ♿ excellent (3 rooms)
- ✖ Felix (p77), Spring Moon (p78)

A Very Close Shave

Among the oft-told tales about the hotel affectionately known as 'the Pen' is the one about the spy in the soup. After the capitulation of British forces in Hong Kong to the Japanese on Christmas Day 1941, it was learned that the manager of the hotel barbershop had been a Japanese spy (and naval commander to boot) – taking advantage of the chatty, informal atmosphere of the surrounds to collect useful information about the troop movements and so on.

A spy with style? The sort of clientele who frequent 'the Pen'

MAN MO TEMPLE (4, A3)

This busy temple is one of the oldest and most famous in Hong Kong. The Man Mo (literally 'civil and martial') is dedicated to two deities. The civil deity is a Chinese statesman of the 3rd century BC called Man Cheung,

INFORMATION
- ☎ 2540 0350
- ✉ 124-126 Hollywood Rd, Sheung Wan
- $ free
- ☽ 8am-6pm
- 🚌 26
- ✖ Boca (p70)

who is worshipped as the god of literature and represented holding a writing brush. The military deity is Kwan Yu, a soldier born in the 2nd century AD and now venerated as the red-cheeked god of war; he is holding a sword. Also known as Kwan Tai, this god's popularity in Hong Kong is probably more attributable to his status as the patron of restaurateurs, pawnbrokers, the police and members of secret societies such as the Triads.

Outside the entrance are four gilt plaques on poles that are carried at procession time. Two plaques describe the gods being worshipped; the others request quietness and respect and warn menstruating women to keep out of the main hall. Inside the temple are two antique chairs shaped like houses, used to carry the two gods at festival time. The coils suspended from the roof are incense cones burned as offerings by worshippers.

The exact date of the temple's construction has never been agreed on, but it's certain it was already standing when the British arrived to claim the island. The present structure was renovated in the mid-19th century.

The Wong Hotel
The area around the Man Mo Temple was used for location shots in the 1960 film the *World of Suzie Wong,* based on the novel by Richard Mason. The building to the right of the temple appears as Suzie's hotel, although the real hotel Luk Kwok (called Nam Kok in the film and now rebuilt) is, of course, in what was then the red-light district of Wan Chai.

NATHAN RD (3, C9)

From Hong Kong Harbour all the way north to Boundary St, Kowloon's border with the New Territories, Nathan Rd is packed with hundreds of shops, hotels and people. It's loud, crowded, relentless and, with dozens of buses juddering along its length, rather asphyxiating.

Kowloon's main drag was named after Sir Matthew Nathan, governor of Hong Kong from 1904 to 1907. Since Kowloon at the time was sparsely populated and such a wide road was thought unnecessary, it was promptly dubbed 'Nathan's Folly'. Nearly all the banyan trees that once lined the street are gone; the few remaining ones are in front of Kowloon Park.

The southern end of Nathan Rd is known as the **Golden Mile**, reflecting both property prices in this high-rent area and the success of the retail trade. Ramshackle blocks stacked with seedy guesthouses awkwardly rub shoulders with top-end hotels; touts sell fake 'copy watch' and pirated DVDs; tailors ply their trade on street corners; and the pavements are chock-a-block with consumers scurrying from one shop to another. Anyone who chooses to stay at the **Holiday Inn Golden Mile** (p98) will have this frenetic scene on their doorstep.

INFORMATION

- 🚌 1, 1A, 6, 6A, 7
- ⛴ Star Ferry
- Ⓜ Tsim Sha Tsui, Jordan, Yau Ma Tei, Mong Kok
- ✕ Tsim Sha Tsui (p76), Yau Ma Tei & Mong Kok (p79)

DON'T MISS

- A sundowner at the Sky Lounge (p85)
- Chinese bric-a-brac at Yue Hwa (p58)
- A shady rest in Kowloon Park (p33)
- A detour to Yuen Po St Bird Garden & Flower Market (p35)

Chungking Mansions

Say 'Hong Kong budget accommodation' and people think of Chungking Mansions, a ramshackle warren of hostels and cheap guesthouses at 36-44 Nathan Rd. All needs can be catered for here – from finding a bed and a curry to getting your hair cut – but you may be put off by the undercurrent of sleaze and the peculiar odour of cooking fat, incense and sewage. The building's infamy is fuelled by tales both tall and true of conflagrations, crimes and unclaimed bodies.

TEN THOUSAND BUDDHAS MONASTERY (1, C1)

It may not be as grand as Indonesia's Borobudur or as old as Cambodia's Angkor Wat, but the Ten Thousand Buddhas Monastery typifies Hong Kong for its deep spirituality, open opulence and more than a hint of absurdity.

INFORMATION

- ☎ 2691 1067
- 💻 www.10kbuddhas.org
- 💲 free (donation requested)
- 🕙 9am-5pm
- 🚆 Sha Tin KCR East Rail

Spiritual hierarchy?

Founded in 1951 and completed six years late, the monastery sits on a hillside about 500m northwest of the Sha Tin KCR East Rail station. It's a relatively steep walk to the monastery grounds, but you'll pass a traditional village, pockets of lush forest and dozens of life-size Buddhist arhats (saints who have eradicated all passions and desires) lining the 400 steps up.

You'll discover the evidence behind the monastery's understated name upon entering the main temple: some **12,800 miniature statues** line the towering walls of the room. Look closely and you'll see that the pose of each figure differs slightly. There are also several other temples, pavilions and a nine-storey **pagoda** on the grounds.

To reach the complex from the Sha Tin KCR East Rail station, take exit B and walk down the ramp, passing a series of traditional village houses on the left. Take a left onto Pai Tau St, but don't mistake the modern Po Fook Hill temple complex at the end of it as your destination. Instead, turn right onto Sheung Wo Che St, passing some government buildings on the left. At the end of the road, a series of signs in English will direct you to the left along a concrete path and through bamboo groves to the start of the steps.

Gold Finger Etcetera

Within the main temple of the Ten Thousand Buddhas Monastery is the embalmed body of the Yuet Kai (1878–1965), the monastery's founder. After he died, his corpse was encased in gold leaf and is now on display under glass. Put a donation in the box next to the display case to help pay for the temple's – and Yuet's – upkeep.

HONG KONG PARK (4, D5)

This is one of the most unusual parks in the world, deliberately designed to look anything but natural, and emphasising artificial creations such as its fountain plaza, conservatory, aviary, fake waterfall, indoor games hall, playground, viewing tower, museum and t'ai chi garden. For all its artifice, though, the 8-hectare park is beautiful in its own weird way, and with a wall of skyscrapers on one side and mountains on the other, it makes for some dramatic photography.

The best feature of the park is the **Edward Youde Aviary**, which is named after a much loved governor (1982–87) who died suddenly in office. Home to more than 600 birds representing some 90 different species, it's a huge and very natural-feeling place. Visitors walk along a wooden bridge suspended some 10m above the ground and on eye-level with the tree branches. The **Forsgate Conservatory** on the slope overlooking the park is the largest in Southeast Asia.

At the park's northernmost tip is the **Flagstaff House Museum of Tea Ware** (p26), built in 1846 and the oldest colonial building still standing in its original spot in Hong Kong. It contains a collection of antique Chinese tea ware – bowls, teaspoons, brewing trays and teapots made of porcelain or purple clay from Yixing. The **KS Lo Gallery** (p26), in a small building to the southeast of the tea ware museum, contains rare Chinese ceramics and stone seals collected by the eponymous benefactor.

INFORMATION

- ☎ park 2521 5041; museum & gallery 2869 0690
- 🖥 http://www.lcsd .gov.hk/parks/hkp /en/index.php
- ✉ 19 Cotton Tree Dr, Admiralty
- 💲 free
- 🕐 park 6.30am–11pm, conservatory & aviary 9am–5pm, museum & gallery 10am–5pm Wed-Mon
- 🚌 3B, 12M, 23, 23B, 40, 103
- ♿ good
- 🍴 restaurant & snack shops on site

Roller-girl in Hong Kong Park

DON'T MISS

- Steaming up in the conservatory's Humid Plant House
- Exploring the canopy with the birds
- Striking a pose in t'ai chi
- Dining at the lakeside restaurant

HAPPY VALLEY RACECOURSE (5, A5)

Although Hong Kong residents can play the Mark Six lottery and bet on football fixtures, horse racing is worth more than US$1 billion annually and remains the most popular form of gambling. The first horse races were held in 1846 at the Happy Valley Racecourse and became an annual event. Now there are about 80 meetings a year split between Happy Valley and the newer and larger course at Sha Tin in the New Territories. The racing season runs from September to late June, with most race meetings taking place on Wednesday evening in Happy Valley and on Saturday afternoon at Sha Tin.

INFORMATION
- ☎ 2895 1523, 2966 8111
- 🖥 www.happyvalley racecourse.com
- ✉ 2 Sports Rd, Happy Valley
- 💲 public stand $10, members' box $50
- 🕐 7pm-11pm Wed, Sat & Sun Sep-Jun
- 🚌 1, 5A (racecourse); 75, 90, 97 (museum)
- Ⓜ Causeway Bay, exit A
- 🚇 Happy Valley
- ♿ Toilets & seating
- ✕ Global Forever Green Taiwanese Restaurant (p74)

If you've been in Hong Kong for less than 21 days you can get a tourist ticket. This is worthwhile, especially when the racecourse is crowded, as tourist ticket-holders are always admitted. Make sure to bring along your passport.

If you know nothing about horseracing, consider joining one of two **Come Horseracing Tours** available from the **Hong Kong Tourist Board** (☎ 2508 1234; www.discoverhongkong.com) during the racing season.

Racing buffs can visit the **Hong Kong Racing Museum** (☎ 2966 8065; www.hkjc.com/english/museum/mu02_index.htm; 2nd fl, Happy Valley Stand, Wong Nai Chung Rd, Happy Valley; admission free; 🕐 10am-5pm Tue-Sun, 10am-12.30pm on race days), which has eight galleries and a cinema showcasing the past 150 years. The most important event in the history of the Happy Valley racetrack – individual winnings notwithstanding – was the huge fire in 1918 that killed hundreds of people. Many of the victims were buried in the **cemeteries** surrounding the track.

Slappers Beware

You can hug them, kiss them and buy them a drink, but whatever you do don't slap or grab the shoulders of your fellow punters. The fickle finger of fate hovers above most endeavours in Hong Kong, including (or especially) gambling. 'Shouldering affection' is a serious no-no and will bring bad luck to the slappee.

HONG KONG TRAIL (2, B2)

The challenging 50km-long Hong Kong Trail allows you to tramp almost the entire length of the island in eight stages. From the upper-level terminus of the Peak Tram on Victoria Peak, the trail follows Lugard Rd to the north, and drops down the hill to Pok Fu Lam Reservoir above Aberdeen, before turning east and zigzagging across the ridges. The trail traverses four country parks: 270-hectare **Pok Fu Lam Country Park** (2, A2), south of Victoria Peak; 423-hectare **Aberdeen Country Park** (2, B3), east of the Peak; 1315-hectare **Tai Tam Country Park** (2, B2) on the eastern side of the island; and **Shek O Country Park** (2, C3), over 700 hectares, in the southeast. Tai Tam is the most beautiful of the four, with its dense emerald forests and trickling streams. The Hong Kong Trail skirts the northern side of the Tai Tam Reservoir, the largest body of water on the island.

It's possible to hike the entire trail in one day (a full 15 hours), but most walkers pick a section to suit their schedule and degree of fitness. For example the last stage, the spectacular Dragon's Back Trail (8.5km, 2¾ hours), starts at To Te Wan and finishes at Big Wave Bay, 2km north of Shek O.

For more information, get a copy of the 1:15000 *Hong Kong Trail* map, published by the Country & Marine Parks Authority and available from the Government Publications Office.

INFORMATION

- 🖳 http://parks.afcd .gov.hk/newparks /eng/index.htm
- ⓘ Country & Marine Parks Authority (☎ 2420 0529); Government Publications Office (4, D4; ☎ 2537 1910; Rm 402, 4th fl, Murray Bldg, 22 Garden Rd, Central)
- 🚍 Peak section (No 1): 15 from Exchange Sq to Victoria Peak; Tai Tam section (No 6): 6 & 61 from Exchange Sq to Wong Nai Chung Gap; Shek O section (No 8): 9 from Shau Kei Wan MTR, 309 from Exchange Sq Sun only
- ♿ toilets & accessible barbecues at Aberdeen Country Park Visitors Centre
- ✕ Peak Lookout (p72); Cafe Deco (p71); Mövenpick Marché (p71)

DON'T MISS

- Views from the Dragon's Back over the South China Sea
- 200 species of butterfly
- Trying your hand at frog-spotting
- 500-year-old lichen in Pok Fu Lam Country Park
- Barking deer in the Tai Tam Valley

Sights & Activities

MUSEUMS

See also the Hong Kong Museum of History (p13).

Flagstaff House Museum of Tea Ware (4, E4)
At the northern end of Hong Kong Park (p23), the oldest colonial building (1846) still standing in Hong Kong houses a collection of antique Chinese tea ware dating back as far as the Western Zhou period (11th to 8th century BC). The **KS Lo Gallery** wing southeast of the tea ware museum contains rare Chinese ceramics and stone seals collected by the eponymous benefactor.
☎ 2869 0690 ☐ www .lcsd.gov.hk/ce/Museum /Arts/english/tea/intro /eintro.html ✉ 10 Cotton Tree Dr, Admiralty ⑤ free ☒ 10am-5pm Wed-Mon Ⓜ Admiralty (exit C1) 🚻 Yes ♿ good/excellent

Hong Kong Heritage Museum (1, C1)
Housed in a mock-traditional building, this award-winning museum has magnificent displays on Cantonese opera, the cultural heritage of the New Territories, a Children's Discovery Gallery with learning and play zones, and a gallery for the impressive art collection of Dr TT Tsui. There are five thematic galleries.
☎ 2180 8188 ☐ www .heritagemuseum.gov.hk ✉ 1 Man Lam Rd, Sha Tin ⑤ $10/5 (free Wed) ☒ 10am-6pm Mon & Wed-Sat, 10am-7pm Sun ⊕ Sha Tin KCR East Rail (then 10min walk west & south along Tai Po Rd & Lion Rock Tunnel Rd) ♿ excellent

Hong Kong Museum of Art (3, C9)
This museum does a good job with classical Chinese art, showcases paintings and lithographs of old Hong Kong in the Historical Pictures Gallery, and focuses mostly on calligraphy in the Xubaizhi collection. There are creditable international exhibitions, but the gallery falls short on contemporary art.
☎ 2721 0116 ☐ www .lcsd.gov.hk/hkma ✉ 10 Salisbury Rd, Tsim Sha Tsui ⑤ $10/5 (free Wed) ☒ 10am-6pm Fri-Wed 🚢 Star Ferry (Tsim Sha Tsui) Ⓜ Tsim Sha Tsui ♿ excellent

Hong Kong Museum of Coastal Defence (2, C2)
The history of Hong Kong's coastal defence is presented in the restored Lei Yue Mun Fort (1887). Exhibitions in the old Redoubt cover the Ming and Qing dynasties, the colonial years, the Japanese invasion and the return of Hong Kong to Chinese sovereignty. There's a historical trail through casemates, tunnels and observation posts.
☎ 2569 1500 ☐ www .lcsd.gov.hk/CE/Museum /Coastal/index.html ✉ 175 Tung Hei Rd, Shau Kei Wan ⑤ $10/5 (free Wed) ☒ 10am-5pm Fri-Wed 🚌 84 Ⓜ Shau

Kei Wan (exit B2, then 15min walk north along Tung Hei Rd)

Hong Kong Museum of Medical Sciences (4, A3)

This small museum of medical implements and accoutrements is less interesting for its exhibits than for its architecture. It is housed in what was once the Old Pathological Institute, a breezy Edwardian-style brick-and-tiled structure built in 1905. The exhibits comparing Chinese and Western approaches to medicine are unusual and instructive.

☎ 2549 5123 🖳 www .hkmms.org.hk ✉ 2 Caine Lane, Mid-Levels 💲 $10/5 🕑 10am-5pm Tue-Sat, 1-5pm Sun 🚌 3B, 23, 23B, 40, 40M, 103, minibus (Star Ferry & GPO)

Hong Kong Planning & Infrastructure Exhibition Gallery (4, E3)

This gallery in the Lower Block Hong Kong City Hall will awaken the Meccano set builder in more than a few visitors. It takes the visitor on an 18.5m 3D 'walk' past recent, ongoing and future civil engineering, urban renewal and environment improvement projects. There are lots of hands-on displays for the kids.

☎ 3101 6516 🖳 www .gov.hk/infrastructure-gallery ✉ 3 Edinburgh Place, Central 💲 free 🕑 10am-6pm Wed-Mon ⛴ Star Ferry (Central) Ⓜ Central (exit K) ♿ good

Hong Kong Science Museum (3, D7)

The Science Museum is a multilevel complex with more than 500 displays on computers, energy, physics, robotics, telecommunications, health and much more. Though some of the exhibits are beginning to look a little dated after 15 years or so, all the buttons to push and robot arms to operate will keep young (and some older) visitors entertained.

☎ 2732 3232 🖳 www .lcsd.gov.hk/CE/Museum /Science ✉ 2 Science Museum Rd, Tsim Sha Tsui East 💲 $25/12.50 (free Wed) 🕑 1-9pm Mon-Wed & Fri, 10am-9pm Sat & Sun 🚌 5, 5C, 8 Ⓜ Tsim Sha Tsui (exit A2) ♿ good

Hong Kong Museums Pass

The Hong Kong Museums Pass (admission 7 days $30, adult/senior & student 6 months $50/25, 1 year $100/50) allows multiple entries to six of Hong Kong's museums: Hong Kong Museum of Coastal Defence, Hong Kong Science Museum, Hong Kong Museum of History, Hong Kong Museum of Art and Hong Kong Space Museum (excluding the Space Theatre) and the Hong Kong Heritage Museum. They are available from any Hong Kong Tourism Board (HKTB) outlet (see p119) or the participating museums themselves.

Need a break from museums? Seek out the sculpture sanctuaries of one of the city's parkland pockets

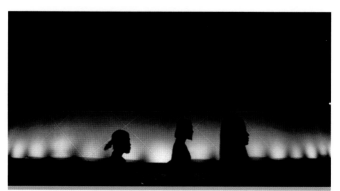

Spaced out: visitors leaving the Hong Kong Space Museum

Hong Kong Space Museum (3, C9)

Just east of the Kowloon Cultural Centre, this golf ball–shaped building consists of the Hall of Space Science, the Hall of Astronomy and the large Space Theatre planetarium. Exhibits include a lump of moon rock, rocket-ship models and NASA's 1962 *Mercury* space capsule. The Space Theatre screens 'sky shows' and IMAX films in English and Cantonese; only children aged three and over are allowed in. ☎ 2721 0226 🖥 www .lcsd.gov.hk/CE/Museum /Space ✉ 10 Salisbury Rd, Tsim Sha Tsui 💲 museum $10/5 (free Wed), theatre from $24/12 ☽ museum 1-9pm Mon & Wed-Fri, 10am-9pm Sat & Sun, theatre 1.30-8.30pm 🚢 Star Ferry (Tsim Sha Tsui) Ⓜ Tsim Sha Tsui ♿ excellent

Hong Kong University Museum & Art Gallery (2, A2)

This museum to the left of Hong Kong University's main building houses ceramics, bronzes, paintings and carvings. Exhibits range from mirrors from the Warring States period through to modern abstracts. There's an intriguing display of crosses made by Nestorians, a Christian sect that arose in Syria and ventured to China during the 13th and 14th centuries. ☎ 2241 5500 🖥 www .hku.hk/hkumag ✉ Fung Ping Shan Bldg, 94 Bonham Rd, Pok Fu Lam 💲 free ☽ 9.30am-6pm Mon-Sat, 1.30pm-5.30pm Sun 🚌 3B, 40, 40M, 103 ♿ good

Law Uk Folk Museum (2, C2)

The small Law Uk Folk Museum is housed in two restored Hakka village houses. In the main building there is an interesting collection of rod puppets and miniature theatre sets. The farmhouses in the courtyard have been kitted out with simple but charming furniture, household items and some farming implements. ☎ 2896 7006 🖥 www .lcsd.gov.hk/CE/Museum /History/en/luf.php ✉ 14 Kut Shing St, Chai Wan 💲 free ☽ 10am-1pm & 2-6pm Mon-Wed, Fri & Sat, 1-6pm Sun Ⓜ Chai Wan (exit B)

Lei Cheng Uk Han Tomb Museum (2, A1)

This burial vault dating from the Eastern Han dynasty (AD 25–220) and central to the museum was discovered in 1955 when workers were levelling the hillside for a housing estate. The tomb is encased in a concrete shell for protection and you can only peek through a plastic window. The museum also contains some 58 pottery and bronze pieces taken from the tomb. ☎ 2386 2863 🖥 http:// www.lcsd.gov.hk/CE /Museum/History/en /lcuht.php ✉ 41 Tonkin St, Sham Shui Po 💲 free ☽ 10am-1pm & 2-6pm Mon-Wed, Fri & Sat, 1-6pm Sun Ⓜ Cheung Sha Wan (exit A3, then 10min northeast along Tonkin St) 🚌 2

GALLERIES

Cattle Depot Artist Village (2, B2)

This erstwhile slaughter-house in far-flung To Kwa Wan is home to local artists who live, work and exhibit in the old abattoir. It's pot-luck but there's always something showing; try the Artist Commune exhibition hall, or Videotage, a non-profit interdisciplinary group of artists based here that concentrates on video and other electronic media.
☎ 2104 3322, 2573 1869 ✉ 63 Ma Tau Kok Rd, To Kwa Wan $ free 🕙 2-8pm Tue-Sun 🚌 3B, 5C, 12A, 21, 61X, 85A, 106 ♿ fair

Fringe Gallery (6, C3)

This all-purpose gallery-cum-bar offers an eclectic klatch of exhibitions (primarily of contemporary fine art) throughout the year. Two other venues in the same building, the Economist Gallery and the Volkswagen fotogalerie, focus on photography, both as storyteller and art form.
☎ 2521 7251 🖥 www .hkfringeclub.com ✉ Ground fl, Fringe Club, 2 Lower Albert Rd, Central $ free 🕙 noon-midnight Mon-Thu, noon-3am Fri & Sat 🚌 13, 23A, 26 Ⓜ Central (exit G)

Hanart TZ Gallery (4, D4)

One of the most influential and innovative galleries in Hong Kong, Hanart shows contemporary Chinese art with a thoroughbred stable of figurative and conceptual painters, sculptors and video artists.
☎ 2526 9019 🖥 tzchang@hanart .com ✉ Rm 202, 2nd fl, Henley Bldg, 5 Queen's Rd Central $ free 🕙 10am-6.30pm Mon-Fri, 10am-6pm Sat Ⓜ Central (exit K) 🚗 Yes ♿ good

John Batten Gallery (6, A2)

Small gallery charged with the enthusiasm and vision of its namesake director. Batten shows local and international painting, photography and video art of consistently high quality.
☎ 2854 1018 🖥 www .johnbattengallery.com ✉ 64 Peel St, Soho $ free 🕙 1-7pm Tue-Sat, 2-5pm Sun 🚌 3B, 40, 40M, 103

Pao Galleries (7, A2)

This major contemporary art gallery in the Hong Kong Arts Centre (p91) has room to host retrospectives and group shows in all visual media. The curatorial vision is lively without being too provocative.
☎ 2824 5330 🖥 www .hkac.org.hk ✉ 2 Harbour Rd, Wan Chai $ free 🕙 10am-8pm (during exhibitions) Ⓜ Wan Chai (exit A5) ♿ good

Sculpture Sanctuary

If you can't face another moment of Nathan Rd's dirt, din and touting tailors, chill out among the artwork of Kowloon Park's **Sculpture Walk** (3, C7). Sprinkled among the greenery are about 30 marble and bronze sculptures by both local and overseas artists. Keep an eye open for the late Antonio Mak's *Torso* and *Concept of Newton* by Scotland's Sir Eduardo Paolozzi. **Salisbury Gardens** (3, C9), leading to the entrance of the Hong Kong Museum of Art (p26), is also lined with modern sculptures, all of which are by contemporary Hong Kong sculptors.

Para/Site Art Space (4, A1)

This adventurous, artist-run art space knows no boundaries when it comes to mixing media. Most art on display is Chinese but there are occasional exhibitions by Westerners. There's a small, finger-on-the-pulse collection of art books and catalogues for sale.

☎ 2517 4620 🖳 www.para-site.org.hk ✉ 4 Po Yan St, Sheung Wan 💲 free 🕒 noon-7pm Wed-Sun 🚌 26 Ⓜ Sheung Wan (exit A2)

Plum Blossoms (6, B2)

Though very much a commercial concern (the late Rudolf Nureyev used to buy his baubles here and other celebrities continue to do so), this gallery is one of the most exquisite and well-established galleries in Hong Kong.

☎ 2521 2189 🖳 www.plumblossoms.com ✉ Ground fl, Chinachem Hollywood Centre, 1-19 Hollywood Rd, Central 💲 free 🕒 10am-6.30pm Mon-Sat Ⓜ Central (exit D2) 🚌 13, 26

Shanghai St Artspace Exhibition Hall (3, B2)

Funded by the Hong Kong Arts Development Council, this exhibition hall is a small space in a strange place and concentrates on cutting-edge new art by local artists. Video assemblages, photography, computer art and mixed media all feature.

☎ 2770 2157 🖳 www.hkadc.org.hk/eng ✉ 404 Shanghai St, Mong Kok 💲 free 🕒 11am-8pm Thu-Tue Ⓜ Yau Ma Tei (exit A1), Mong Kok (exit E1) ♿ fair

Cultural Centre: pretty in pink? Locals aren't convinced

NOTABLE BUILDINGS

See also the iconic Bank of China Tower (p18).

Center (6, B1)

From close up, the protruding corners of this star-shaped, 73-storey building appear to cut into the structure. But what really sets it apart is the hypnotic nightly light show that sends colour lights cascading down the towering 'spines' every 15 minutes. The main visitors' branch of the Hong Kong Tourism Board (HKTB) is here.

✉ 99 Queens Rd Central
$ free **M** Central (exit D) ♿ yes ♿ excellent

Exchange Square (4, D3)

This complex of three elevated office towers is home to the Hong Kong Stock Exchange. Outside Towers I and II is a seating area surrounding a fountain, and several sculptures including one by Henry Moore. Below the square is Central's bus station.

✉ 8 Connaught Place, Central **$** free **M** Central (exit A) ♿ yes

Government House (4, C4)

Parts of the one-time residence of Hong Kong's governors date back to 1856, though the com-

manding tower was added by the Japanese during WWII. The current chief executive, Tung Chee Hwa, refuses to take up residence here, claiming the feng shui isn't satisfactory.

☎ 2530 2003 ✉ Upper Albert Rd, Central **$** free ☽ open one Sun in Mar **M** Central (exit G) 🚌 3B, 12, 23, 103

Hong Kong Convention and Exhibition Centre (7, B1)

This enormous complex, built in 1988 and extended onto reclaimed land for the handover ceremony in June 1997, boasts an enormous 'glass curtain' – a window seven storeys high – facing the harbour. The design of the extension has been compared with a bird in flight, a skate, a banana leaf and a lotus petal.

☎ 2582 8888 🖥 www.hkcec.com ✉ 1 Expo Dr, Wan Chai **$** free 🚌 2A, 8, 40, 40M ⚓ Star Ferry (Wan Chai) **M** Wan Chai (exit A1) ♿ good

Hong Kong Cultural Centre (3, B9)

This odd building clad in pink ceramic tiles is one of

Hong Kong's most distinctive – if not loved – landmarks. Nonetheless the centre is a world-class venue with a 2100-seat concert hall, theatres, rehearsal studios and an impressive main lobby. There are daily tours; phone ahead.

☎ 2734 2009 🖥 www.lcsd.gov.hk/CE/Cultural Service/HKCC/index_e.htm ✉ 10 Salisbury Rd, Tsim Sha Tsui **$** free, tours $10/5 ☽ 9am-11pm ⚓ Star Ferry (Tsim Sha Tsui) **M** Tsim Sha Tsui (exit E) ♿ good

Hong Kong Design Centre (4, D5)

The design centre, just opposite Hong Kong Park, is housed in one of the most graceful colonial buildings (1896) in the territory. Even though it doesn't have any exhibitions open to the public, the exterior and public areas are worth a look.

☎ 2522 8688 🖥 www.hkdesigncentre.org ✉ 28 Kennedy Rd, Mid-Levels **$** free ☽ 9am-6pm (variable) 🚌 12A

Hongkong & Shanghai Bank (4, D4)

This 180m-tall glass and

Not for Long Tall

The IFC (International Finance Centre) Towers were partly designed by Cesar Pelli, the man responsible for Canary Wharf in London. **One IFC** (4, C2), which opened in 1999, is a 'mere' 38 levels tall. At 88 storeys and almost 410m, **Two IFC** (4, D2), topped out in 2003, is Hong Kong's tallest building – at least for the moment. Union Square, a 108-storey development on reclaimed land above the Kowloon MTR and Airport Express station, will claim the distinction in 2007.

aluminium building is an innovative masterpiece. Locals call it the 'Robot Building', because you can see the chains and motors of the escalators and other moving parts whirring away inside. Structurally, the building is equally radical, built on a 'coat-hanger' frame. Stand in the atrium and look up to see how the structure hangs, rather than ascends.

✉ **1 Queen's Rd Central** $ **free** ⏱ **9am-4.30pm Mon-Fri, 9am-12.30pm Sat** Ⓜ **Central (exit K)** 🚻 **yes** ♿ **good**

Jardine House (4, D3)
This 52-storey silver monolith was Hong Kong's first true 'skyscraper' when it opened as the Connaught Centre in 1973. The building's 1750 porthole-like windows have earned it a less respectable Chinese nickname: 'House of 1000 Arseholes'.

✉ **1 Connaught Pl, Central** $ **free** Ⓜ **Central (exit A)** 🚻 **yes** ♿ **fair**

KCR Clock Tower (3, B9)
This 45m-high clock tower, built in 1922, is all that remains of the southern terminus of the Kowloon-Canton Railway, inaugurated in 1916 and torn down in 1978. The original building, which had columns and was colonial in style, was too small to handle the large volume of passenger traffic. Visitors are sometimes allowed into the tower on Sunday from 10am to 6pm.

✉ **Tsim Sha Tsui Public Pier, Salisbury Rd, Tsim Sha Tsui** $ **free** ⛴ **Star Ferry (Tsim Sha Tsui)** Ⓜ **Tsim Sha Tsui (exit E)**

Legislative Council Building (4, D3)
This colonnaded, domed neoclassical building is the old Supreme Court, built in 1910 of granite quarried on Stonecutter Island (2, A1). Standing atop the pediment is a blindfolded statue of Themis, the Greek goddess of justice.

✉ **8 Jackson Rd, Central** $ **free** Ⓜ **Central (exit J1)** 🚻 **yes** ♿ **fair**

Flexible Strength

A sure sign that a building is going up (or coming down) in Hong Kong is the arrival of truckloads of bamboo poles for scaffolding. The poles are lashed together with plastic bindings to form a grid and the structure is then covered in green netting. It may not look very high-tech, but bamboo is lighter, cheaper and more flexible than the bolted steel tubing used by scaffolders in the West. It also copes much better with tensile stress, as you'll see if you watch builders scuttle around in their thin-soled slippers, barely causing a ripple.

A city always on the up...

PARKS & GARDENS

See also Hong Kong Park (p23).

Cheung Kong Park (4, D4)
The sole reason why you might stop and look at this pretty park abutting St John's Cathedral is that developers were required to lay it out when they built 70-storey Cheung Kong Centre immediately to the north. Behind the park is the French Mission building, a charming structure built for the Russian consul in 1868 but extensively rebuilt in 1917. It served as the headquarters of the provisional colonial government after WWII and houses the Court of Final Appeal, the highest judicial body in Hong Kong.
✉ **1 Battery Path, Central** $ **free** Ⓜ **Central (exit K)** ♿ **good**

Hong Kong Zoological & Botanical Gardens (4, C4)
These gardens, established in 1864, are a pleasant assembly of fountains, sculptures, greenhouses, a playground, a zoo and some fabulous aviaries. There are hundreds of species of birds in residence as well as exotic trees, plants and shrubs. The zoo is surprisingly comprehensive and one of the world's leading centres for the captive breeding of endangered species. The gardens are divided by Albany Rd, with the plants and aviaries to the east off Garden Rd, and most of the animals to the west.
☎ **2530 0154** 🖳 **http://www.lcsd.gov.hk/parks/hkzbg/en/index.php** ✉ **Albany Rd, Central** $ **free** ☼ **terrace gardens 6am-10pm, zoo & aviaries 6am-7pm, greenhouses 9am-4.30pm** 🚌 **3B, 12, 40, 40M** Ⓜ **Central (exit G)** ♿ **fair**

Kowloon Park (3, C7)
Built on the site of a barracks for Indian soldiers in the colonial army, Kowloon Park is an oasis of greenery and a refreshing escape from the hustle and bustle of Tsim Sha Tsui. Pathways and walls crisscross the grass, birds hop around

Hong Kong's Own Blossom

The flower on Hong Kong's flag is the *Bauhinia blakeana*, also called the Hong Kong orchid. From early November to March you may see the purple blossoms on bauhinia trees, a species unique to the territory, in **Victoria Park** (p34), **Kowloon Walled City Park** (p34) or outside the **Foreign Correspondents' Club** (6, C3), which is next to the Ice House (p100) in Central.

Braving the elements to spot an orchid

in cages, and towers and viewpoints dot the landscape. The Sculpture Walk features works by local and international sculptors. There's also an excellent (though crowded) indoor/outdoor pool complex complete with waterfalls.

☎ 2724 3344 ⌨ www.lcsd.gov.hk/LEISURE/LM/parks/kp/index.html ✉ 22 Austin Rd, Tsim Sha Tsui $ free ☾ 6am-midnight Ⓜ Tsim Sha Tsui (exit A1), Jordan (exit C1) ♿ good

Kowloon Walled City Park (2, B1)

The walls that enclose this beautiful park were once the perimeter of a notorious village that technically remained part of China throughout British rule. The enclave was known for its vice, prostitution, gambling and – worst of all – illegal dentists. In 1984 the Hong Kong government acquired the area, rehoused the residents elsewhere and replaced them with pavilions, ponds, turtles, goldfish and exquisite flora. The park opened in 1996.

☎ 2716 9962, 2762 2084 ⌨ http://www.lcsd.gov.hk/parks/kwcp/en/index.php ✉ Tung Tsing Rd, Kowloon City $ free ☾ 6.30am-11pm 🚌 1, 10, 113 Ⓜ Lok Fu (exit B, then 15min walk south on Junction & Tung Tau Tsuen Rds) ♿ good

Statue Square (4, D3)

Statue Square once displayed various effigies of British royalty, but these were carted away by the Japanese during WWII. The only statue that remains is the bronze of Sir Thomas Jackson, a particularly successful Victorian-era head of the Hongkong and Shanghai Bank, which he now faces. On the northern side of Chater Rd is the cenotaph dedicated to Hong Kong residents killed during the two world wars.

✉ Chater & Des Voeux Rds, Central Ⓜ Central (exit K) 🚌 yes ♿ good

Victoria Park (5, C3)

At 17 hectares, one of the biggest patches of public greenery in urban Hong Kong, Victoria Park is a popular escape. The best time to stroll around is in the morning on weekdays when it becomes a forest of people practising the slow-motion choreography of t'ai chi. Among the park's unique features is a pebble garden to stroll over and massage your soles and a large swimming pool complex. The park becomes a flower market a few days before the Chinese New Year. It's also worth a visit during the Mid-Autumn (Moon) Festival when people carry lanterns.

☎ 2570 6186 ⌨ www.lcsd.gov.hk/parks/vp/en/index.php ✉ Causeway Rd, Causeway Bay $ free ☾ 24hr Ⓜ Causeway Bay (exit E), Tin Hau (exit A2) 🚌 yes ♿ good

---

Maid in Hong Kong

On Sunday – what they call 'freedom day' – a large percentage of Hong Kong's 153,000 Filipino *amahs* (maids) take over Central's pavements and public spaces, especially pedestrianised Chater Rd and **Statue Square** (4, D3). They come in groups to share food, gossip, play cards, do one another's hair and even pray together. The territory's 65,000 Indonesian maids tend to converge on **Victoria Park** (5, C3) on the same day for picnics and impromptu soccer matches.

Solving the world's problems

MARKETS

See also the Temple St Night Market (p16).

Cat St Market (4, A2)
Upper Lascar Row is the official name of Cat St, a pedestrian-only laneway lined with antique and curio shops and stalls selling found objects, cheap jewellery, ornaments, carvings and newly minted ancient coins. It's a fun place to trawl through for a trinket or two but expect more rough than diamonds.
✉ Upper Lascar Row, Sheung Wan ⏱ 9am-6pm Ⓜ Sheung Wan (exit A2)

Jade Market (3, B4)
This market, split into two parts by the loop formed by Battery St, has hundreds of stalls selling all varieties and grades of jade. Unless you really know your nephrite from your jadeite, it's not wise to buy expensive pieces here.
✉ Kansu & Battery Sts, Yau Ma Tei ⏱ 10am-4pm 🚌 9 Ⓜ Yau Ma Tei (exit C), Jordan (exit A) ♿ good

Stanley Market (2, B3)
No big bargains nor big stings, just reasonably priced casual clothes (plenty of large sizes), bric-a-brac, toys and formulaic art, all in a nicely confusing maze of alleys running down to Stanley Bay. It's best to go during the week; at the weekend the market is bursting at the seams with both tourists and locals alike.
✉ off Stanley Village Rd, Stanley ⏱ 9am-6pm 🚌 6, 6A, 6X, 260 ♿ fair

Tung Choi St Market (3, C1)
Also known as Ladies' Market, the Tung Choi St market is a cheek-by-jowl affair offering up cheap clothes and trinkets. Vendors start setting up their stalls as early as noon, but it's best to get here between 1pm and 6pm when there's much more on offer.
✉ Tung Choi St (btwn Argyle & Dundas Sts), Mong Kok ⏱ noon-10.30pm Ⓜ Mong Kok (exit D3)

Western Market (4, B2)
Opposite Central's Macau ferry terminal, this three-storey Edwardian building (1906), was reopened in 1991 as a shopping centre. It's filled with modern shops selling curios and small antiques, embroideries and collectibles. The 1st floor has piece goods for the most part, and some decent silks can be bought here.
✉ 323 Des Voeux Rd Central & New Market St, Sheung Wan ⏱ 10am-7pm Ⓜ Sheung Wan (exit C) 🚋 yes

Yuen Po St Bird Garden (2, B1)
There are hundreds of birds for sale at this market, along with elaborate cages carved from teak and bamboo. The Chinese have long favoured songbirds as pets. In fact a bird's singing prowess often determines its price. Some birds are also considered harbingers of good fortune, which is why they are sometimes taken to the races.
✉ Yuen Po Street (btwn Boundary St & Flower Market Rd), Mong Kok ⏱ 7am-8pm 🚌 1, 1A, 2C, 12A Ⓜ Prince Edward (exit B1) 🚋 Mong Kok KCR East Rail ♿ fair

Pet or petit hors d'oeuvre...

PLACES OF WORSHIP

See also Po Lin (p14), Man Mo Temple (p20) and Ten Thousand Buddhas Monastery (p22).

Ahh the serenity: Chi Lin Nunnery

Chi Lin Nunnery (2, B1)

This Tang-style wooden complex, built in 1998, is a serene place with lotus ponds, bonsai, and silent nuns delivering offerings to Buddha and arhats. Designed to show the harmony of humans with nature, it's convincing until you spy the nearby high-rises.

☎ 2354 1604 ✉ 5 Chi Lin Dr, Diamond Hill 💲 free 🕙 nunnery 9am-4pm Thu-Tue, garden 6.30am-7pm Ⓜ Diamond Hill (exit C2, then a 5min walk along Fung Tak Rd)

Kowloon Mosque & Islamic Centre (3, C7)

Hong Kong's largest mosque, completed 1984, occupies the site of a previous mosque built in 1896 for Muslim Indian troops garrisoned in barracks at what is now Kowloon Park. The mosque has a handsome dome, minarets and carved marble exterior. Muslims are welcome to attend services but non-Muslims should ask permission to enter. Remember to remove your shoes.

☎ 2724 0095 ✉ 105 Nathan Rd, Tsim Sha Tsui 💲 free 🕙 5am-10pm Ⓜ Tsim Sha Tsui (exit A1)

Ohel Leah Synagogue (4, A3)

This 'Moorish Romantic' temple, completed in 1902, is named after Lea Gubbay Sassoon, matriarch of a wealthy (and philanthropic) Sephardic Jewish family who can trace its roots back to the beginning of the colony. Bring ID if you plan to visit the sumptuous interior.

☎ 2857 6095 🖳 www .ohelleah.org ✉ 70 Robinson Rd, Mid-Levels 💲 free 🕙 10.30am-7pm Mon-Thu (by appointment only) 🚌 3B, 13, 23, 23B, 40

St John's Cathedral (4, D4)

Built in 1847, this Anglican cathedral is now lost in a forest of skyscrapers. It suffered heavy damage during WWII; after the war the front doors were remade using timber salvaged from HMS *Tamar*, a British warship that guarded the entrance to Victoria Harbour, and the beautiful William Morris stained glass replaced.

☎ 2523 4157 🖳 www .stjohnscathedral.org.hk ✉ 4-8 Garden Rd (enter from Battery Path), Central

Sticks in the Know

In the early evening **Wong Tai Sin Temple** (2, B1) is abuzz with people just off work praying and divining the future with *chim* (fortune sticks). The temple is flanked by stacks of bamboo canisters containing the narrow wooden sticks. The routine is to ask a question and shake the canister until one stick falls out. Each stick bears a numeral, which corresponds to a printed slip of paper in a set held by the temple guardian. That slip of paper should be taken to the temple's fortune-teller, who can interpret its particular meaning for you.

$ free ⏰ 7.15am-6.30pm Mon & Tue, 9.30am-5.15pm Wed, 8.30am-1.15pm Thu, 8am-5.30pm Fri & Sat, 8am-6.30pm Sun Ⓜ Central (exit J2) ♿ fair

Tin Hau Temple (3, B4)
A couple of blocks northeast of the Jade Market (p35) is this temple dedicated to Tin Hau, the goddess of seafarers. You'll find a row of fortune tellers, some of whom speak English, through the last doorway on the right from the main entrance on Public Square St. ☎ 2332 9240 ✉ cnr Public Sq St & Nathan Rd, Yau Ma Tei **$** free ⏰ 8am-6pm Ⓜ Yau Ma Tei (exit C)

Wong Tai Sin Temple (2, B1)
This large, very active Taoist temple was built in 1973 and dedicated to the god Wong Tai Sin, who is worshipped by businesspeople, the sick, and those trying to avoid illness. Behind the main temple are the peaceful Good Wish Gardens, with colourful pavilions, bridges, carp ponds and an artificial waterway. ☎ 2854 4333 ✉ Lung Cheung Rd, Wong Tai Sin **$** $2 donation ⏰ 7am-6pm Ⓜ Wong Tai Sin (exit B2)

QUIRKY HONG KONG

Sure, we've all strapped kids to bamboo poles and waved them around in a parade. And who among us hasn't made a half-coffee/half-tea cuppa as a pick-me-up? And of course we all throw oranges up into a tree to give fate a gentle nudge. We just don't do them all on the same day, which is what you can do in Hong Kong.

Going for the Buns
The eight-day Cheung Chau Bun Festival in May is renowned for its bun towers built near **Pak Tai Temple** (p43). These are formed with bamboo scaffolding up to 20m high and covered with sacred rolls. At one time people would scramble up the towers on the designated day to grab one of the buns for good luck; for safety reasons the buns are now just handed out. On the third day of the festival (a Sunday) there's a lively procession of floats, stilt walkers and colourfully dressed 'floating children' who are carried through the streets on long poles, cleverly wired to metal supports hidden under their clothing.

Let the bun festivities begin

Central Escalator (6, A3)
The world's longest outdoor people-mover is part commuter travelator, part sightseeing ride and part pick-up procession. It consists of elevated escalators, moving walkways and linking stairs covering the 800m hill from Central's offices to the bedroom communities of the Mid-Levels. The best part of the ride is gliding by the Shelley St bars; there's just enough time to make flirtatious eye contact with the denizens within. ☎ Cochrane, Shelley & Peel Sts, Central **$** free ⏰ 6-10am (down), 10.20am-midnight (up) 🚌 3B, 12, 23, 23A, 40 Ⓜ Central (exit D) ♿ yes

Lam Tsuen Wishing Tree (1, C1)
If you're crossing your fingers and avoiding the cracks in the pavement but still can't seem to get lucky, pay a visit to the

Lam Tsuen wishing tree, a large banyan laden with, er, oranges northwest of Tai Po. Write your wish on a swatch of paper, tie it to an orange and lob it as high as you can into the tree. If the fruit lodges in the branches, you're in luck, and the higher it goes, the more chance there is of your wish coming true.
✉ **Lam Kam Rd, Lam Tsuen, Fong Ma Po** $ free ☺ 24hr 🚇 Tai Po Market KCR East Rail (then bus 64K)

Lovers' Rock (4, H6)
A kilometre or so west of the Happy Valley Racecourse (p24) lies what the Chinese call *Yan Yuen Sek*, a phallus-shaped boulder on a bluff at the end of a track above Bowen Rd. The site is a favourite pilgrimage destination for childless women and those who think their lovers or husbands (or sons or next-door neighbours...) could use a prayer and a joss stick

or two. It's especially busy during the Maiden's Festival in mid-August.
✉ **off Bowen Rd, Wan Chai Gap** $ free ☺ 24hr 🚌 15, 15B, 315, 515

Noonday Gun (5, B3)
One of the few vestiges of Causeway Bay's colonial past is this 3lb quick-firing cannon built by Hotchkiss of Portsmouth in 1901. It stands opposite the Excelsior Hong Kong hotel (accessible via a tunnel under the road from the World Trade Centre basement, through a door marked 'Car Park Shroff, Marina Club & Noon Gun') and is fired daily at noon. Noel Coward made the gun famous with his satirical song 'Mad Dogs and Englishmen' (1924) about colonists who braved the heat of midday when local people stayed indoors: 'In Hong Kong/they strike a gong/and fire off a noon-day gun/to reprimand each inmate/who's in late'.

✉ **221 Gloucester Rd, Causeway Bay** ☺ subway access 7am-midnight Ⓜ Causeway Bay (exit D1)

Snake King Restaurant (1, B1)
The Chinese are firm believers in the adage 'You are what you eat'. Snake meat, for example, is considered good for the health, especially in cold weather when restaurants put snake soup and other dishes on their menus. Older women drink snake blood because they believe it cures or alleviates arthritis. Some men drink the blood mixed with Chinese wine as an aphrodisiac. If you are in Hong Kong in autumn or winter and are anxious to try some herpetological treats, the Snake King in Kowloon City – one of some 130 snake shops in Hong Kong – can oblige.
☎ 2383 6297 ✉ **11 Lung Kong Rd, Kowloon City** $ $50-220 ☺ 10am-11pm 🚌 5C, 26

Slow Down, Tune In, Chill Out, Tone Up
- **Happy Foot Reflexology Centre** (6, B1; ☎ 2544 1010; 11th & 13th fl, Jade Centre, 98-102 Wellington St, Central; ☺ 10am-midnight) Give your tootsies a pampering at the aptly named Happy Foot. Foot massages start at $198 for 50 minutes.
- **Healing Plants** (6, B2; ☎ 2815 5005; info@ehealingplants.com; 17 Lyndhurst Tce, Central; ☺ 10am-8pm Mon-Sat, noon-7pm Sun) Acupuncture, reflexology, Swedish massage and homeopathic doctors at hand.
- **Q** (6, B3; ☎ 2521 4555; www.q-yoga.com; 3rd fl, Winning Centre, 46-48 Wyndham St, Central; ☺ 7am-9.30pm Mon-Sat) Hong Kong's poshest yoga studio offers hatha and ashtanga classes starting at $1800 for 10 sessions.
- **Yoga Central** (6, C3; ☎ 2982 4308; www.yogacentral.com.hk; 4th fl, 13 Wyndham St, Central; ☺ varies) Offering hatha yoga with an iyengar spin, this established studio has beginner and intermediate classes Monday to Saturday from $120 per hour.

HONG KONG FOR CHILDREN

The upside about bringing children to Hong Kong is that people are tolerant of child-related chaos. Indeed, Hong Kong Chinese indulge their children's every whim up to about school age, at which point they're expected to grow up. There are playgrounds dotted around but there aren't many public parks where you can let the wild things exhaust themselves. That said, the colour and vibrancy of Hong Kong's sights will appeal to children.

Ocean Park (2, B3)

Hong Kong's biggest theme park, with roller coasters, the world's largest aquarium and an Atoll Reef, both amuses and educates. The two-part complex is linked by a scenic (hair-raising) cable-car ride. The park entrance is on the lowland side and the main section is on the headlands, with terrific views of the South China Sea.
☎ 2552 0291
🖳 www.oceanpark.com
.hk ✉ Ocean Park Rd,
Aberdeen 💲 $185/93
🕑 10am-6pm 🚍 6A, 6X,
629 (Ocean Park Citybus),
green minibus 6

Sheung Wan Gala Point (4, A1)

Just west of the Macau ferry terminal, what was for decades known as the 'Poor Man's Nightclub' has been resurrected. It's a night market divided into three zones – shopping, games and dining – and attracts families, couples and young people on a budget.
✉ Chung Kong Rd 💲 free
🕑 6pm-2am Mon-Fri,
11am-2am Sat & Sun
Ⓜ Sheung Wan (exit C)

Teddy Bear Kingdom (3, C9)

Those under-threes who are disappointed with being

> ### Minders in Mind
> Most hotels will be able to recommend babysitters if you have daytime appointments or are considering a night out without the kid(s). Otherwise contact **Rent-a-Mum** (6, B2; ☎ 2523 4868; rentamum@netvigator .com; 12a Amber Lodge, 21-25 Hollywood Rd, Central). Expect to pay between $110 and $160 per hour.

turned away at the Space Theatre (p28) may find some distraction in Teddy Bear Kingdom, the world's first indoor amusement park devoted solely to teddy bears. It's divided into several zones full of faux tropical trees and stuffed beasties, and even has a Teddy Bear Museum with some 400 stuffed cuddlies from around the world.
☎ 2130 2130 🖳 www
.teddybearkingdom.com
.hk ✉ Amazon, 12 Salisbury Rd, Tsim Sha Tsui
💲 Mon-Fri $30/10, Sat & Sun $50/20 🕑 10am-10pm 🚢 Star Ferry (Tsim Sha Tsui) Ⓜ Tsim Sha Tsui (exit E)

A-Z of Kiddie Attractions

Aberdeen Harbour (p49) Seen from a sampan or junk cruise; **Dim Sum** (boxed text p66) A loud, lucky-dip lunch; **Hong Kong Heritage Museum** (p26) A paradise of interactive display; **Hong Kong Park** (p23) Birds, waterfalls and playgrounds; **Hong Kong Science Museum** (p27) Knobs to pull and arms to twist; **Hong Kong Space Museum** (p28) Big-screen entertainment; **Public Transport** (p112) From the hi-tech MTR to lurching trams; **Repulse Bay** (p17) Beach and Buddhist statues; **Star Ferry** (p9) Boating brilliance across the harbour; **Tsim Sha Tsui Promenade** (p12) A nightly light show; **Wong Tai Sin Temple** (p37) Pagodas, pungent incense and pick-up-sticks; **Yuen Po St Bird Garden** (p35) Confab with feathered friends; **Zoological & Botanical Gardens** (p33) Animal overload

Out & About

WALKING TOURS
Central Stroll

Begin at the **Star Ferry pier** (**1**; p113) in Central. With your back to the 2nd-class ferry entrance, Hong Kong's last few rickshaws in front of you and **Hong Kong City Hall** (**2**; p91) to your left, follow the underground walkway to Chater Rd and **Statue Square** (**3**; p34). Cross the square and head east past the **Legislative Council Building** (**4**; p32) to Chater Garden. Cross Garden Rd to the **Bank of China Tower** (**5**; p18). Head east along Queen's Rd Central, under the flyover and on to the **Flagstaff House Museum of Tea Ware** (**6**; p26) in **Hong Kong Park** (**7**; p23). Elevated walkways take you over Cotton Tree Dr, through Citybank Tower, over Garden Rd and through Cheung Kong Park to **St John's Cathedral** (**8**; p36). Take Battery Path down to Queen's Rd Central, cross over and walk east. If you're hungry, **Mix** (**9**; p68) has good sandwiches, salads and juices. Next door is the **Hongkong & Shanghai Bank** (**10**; p31); walk through the ground floor plaza and entrance/exit K to the Central MTR station is on the west side of Statue Square.

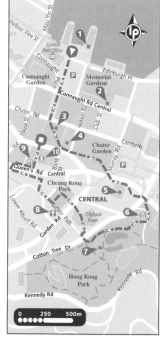

distance 2km **duration** 1hr
► **start**
🚢 Star Ferry
● **end**
Ⓜ Central (entrance/exit K)

By road or by foot? The choice along Battery Path is pretty obvious...

Shuffle to Sheung Wan

Browse the **dried seafood shops** (**1**) of Des Voeux Rd West then turn up Ko Shing St, where there are **herbal medicine wholesalers** (**2**). At the end of the street turn right onto Connaught Rd West to the **Western Market**

Enter at your own risk

---

distance 1.9km **duration** 1hr
▶ **start**
🚋 Kennedy Town
(Sutherland St stop)
◉ **end**
Ⓜ Sheung Wan
(entrance/exit B)

(**3**; p35). Walk south along Morrison St and turn right on Queen's Rd West. Here you'll pass **traditional shops** (**4**) selling bird's nests (for soup) and paper offerings for the dead. Across Queen's Rd Central is **Possession St** (**5**), where the Union Jack Flag first flew in 1841. Ascending Pound Lane to where it meets Tai Ping Shan St, look to the right to spot **Pak Sing Ancestral Hall** (**6**), originally a storeroom for bodies awaiting burial in China. Descend Upper Station St to Hollywood Rd's **antique shops** (**7**; p52). Continuing east on Hollywood Rd brings you to **Man Mo Temple** (**8**; p20). Take a short hop down Ladder St to Upper Lascar Row, home of **Cat St Market** (**9**; p35). Ladder St brings you to Queen's Rd Central. Cross it and follow Hillier St to Bonham Strand. Head east to **Man Wa Lane** (**10**) where you'll find traditional carved chops (seals) for sale. Due north is the **Korea Garden restaurant** (**11**; p70) and, just west, the Sheung Wan MTR (entrance/exit B).

March Through Mong Kok

Take exit A from Prince Edward MTR, walk north up Nathan Rd, then turn right onto Boundary St. **Yuen Po St Bird Garden** (**1**; p35) is a 10-minute walk away. Continue to the daily **Flower Market** (**2**) where some 50 florists sell blooms and plants. At the end of the street, turn left onto Sai Yee St, then right onto Prince Edward Rd West. At Tung Choi St turn left to find **shops** (**3**) selling goldfish (important in feng shui), and bicycles. South of Argyle St is the Tung Choi St Market, also known as the **Ladies' Market** (**4**; p35). Turn right at Dundas St; the **Trendy Zone mall** (**5**; p61) is on the corner of Nathan Rd. Cross over and turn left into Shanghai St where you'll find the **Shanghai St Artspace Exhibition Hall** (**6**; p30). Cut down Hi Lung Lane to Temple St; **Temple St Night Market** (**7**; p16) runs down to Jordan Rd, separated by **Tin Hau Temple** (**8**; p37) and, to the west, the **Jade Market** (**9**; p35). If you want to take a load off your feet, see what's showing at the **Broadway Cinematheque** (**10**; p88) or have something warm and/ or sweet at the attached Kubrick Bookshop Cafe (p80).

distance 4.5km **duration** 2hr
▶ **start**
Ⓜ Prince Edward
(entrance/exit A)
◉ **end**
Ⓜ Jordan (entrance/exit A)

Night Light

Festive they may appear to be, but the pink-and-green neon strip lights you'll see hanging above Mong Kok's streets are pointing to brothels, and you'll see a lot of hotels advertising rooms by the hour. Though there's no appreciable rise in street crime in this seedy part of Hong Kong, Mong Kok is best avoided after midnight.

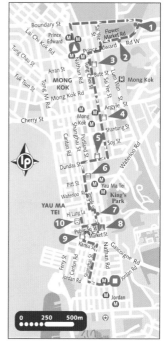

Cheung Chau Canter

Disembark from the ferry and turn left, past Praya St's seafood **restaurants** (**1**) and houseboats in the harbour facing Pak She Praya Rd. Turn right into Pak She Fourth Lane to **Pak Tai Temple** (**2**; boxed text p37), site of the colourful Bun Festival in May. Head south along Pak She St and dogleg into San Hing St, past **shops** (**3**) selling paper offerings, herbs and incense. Turn left at Tung Wan Rd: the **Hometown Teahouse** (**4**; ☎ 2981 5038; 12 Tung Wan Rd; ⏰ noon-midnight) is a great place for a snack and a cuppa. **Tung Wan Beach** (**5**) at the end of the street is popular with windsurfers and swimmers. Walk south along the shore to the **Warwick Hotel** (**6**); in front are some rock carvings dating back 3000 years. Head up Cheung Chau Sports Rd behind the hotel, then right onto Kwun Yam Wan Rd. Past the sports ground you'll come to **Kwan Kung Pavilion** (**7**), dedicated to Kwan Yu (or Kwan Tai), god of war and righteousness. Turn left out

of the temple onto Peak Rd, which leads along a scenic ridge, past the island's cemetery and down to the **Sai Wan** (**8**) ferry pier. From here a path leads westward to **Cheung Po Tsai Cave** (**9**), which was an old pirate hideout. Return to Cheung Chau village either by *kaido* (small boat; $3/2) or on foot along Sai Wan Rd (20 to 30 minutes).

A floating abode in Cheung Chau harbour

---

distance 4.5km **duration** 2½hr
▶ **start**
   🚢 Cheung Chau village
   (from Central)
◉ **end**
   🚢 Sai Wan pier
   (to Cheung Chau village)

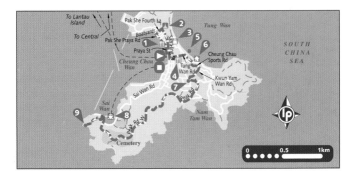

DAY TRIPS
Lantau Island   (1, B3)

Measuring some 144 sq km, Lantau is almost twice the size of Hong Kong Island, and more than half of this sparsely populated mountainous island – 78.5 sq km, in fact – is country parkland. There are good hikes, excellent beaches, and interesting villages and monasteries nestled in the hills.

A worthwhile five- to six-hour trip can be made by taking the ferry to **Mui Wo** then bus 2 to the Buddhist monastery **Po Lin** in Ngong Ping and the awesome **Tian Tan Buddha Statue** (p14). From here catch bus 21 to the fishing town of **Tai O** on Lantau's west coast, where traditional stilt houses can still be seen. Jump on the anachronistic **rope-tow ferry** that connects the island town to the mainland, and at the Fook Lam Moon restaurant turn right to visit the 15th-century **Kwan Tai temple** on Kat Hing St. From Tai O take bus 1 back to Mui Wo or bus 11 over the steep interior to **Tung Chung**, where you'll see how much a village can change when an international airport is plonked down beside it. There's an MTR station at Tung Chung to take you back to the city.

If you're keen for a dip, hop off bus No 1 (en route to Mui Wo) at **Cheung Sha**, a 3km sandy stretch divided into Lower Cheung Sha and the prettier Upper Cheung Sha. Bus No 4 will get you here from Mui Wo.

The 70km-long **Lantau Trail** loops around the island from Mui Wo. The scenic middle section is accessible from Po Lin Monastery. It's 17.5km (or seven hours) from Ngong Ping to Mui Wo, via Lantau and Sunset Peaks. **Hong Kong Disneyland** is slated to open on reclaimed land off the northeast coast of the island in 2006.

> **INFORMATION**
> *20-30km west of Central*
> 🚢 Central/Tsim Sha Tsui to Mui Wo
> Ⓜ Tung Chung
> 💲 ferry $10.50-31, bus $4-25, MTR $23
> ⓘ New World First Ferry (☎ 2131 8181; www.nwff.com.hk); Country & Marine Parks Authority (☎ 2420 0529; http://parks.afcd .gov.hk)
> ✕ Vegetarian restaurant, Po Lin Monastery, Ngong Ping; Fook Lam Moon, 29 Tai O Market St, Tai O (seafood); Stoep, 32 Lower Cheung Sha Village (beachfront Mediterranean)

Light a joss stick or have your fortune read at Po Lin Monastery

Stanley (2, C3)

About 2000 people lived at Stanley when the British took control in 1841, making it one of Hong Kong Island's largest settlements at the time. A prison was built near the village in 1937 – just in time for the Japanese to intern the builders. Stanley Prison is a maximum security facility today.

The main attraction here is **Stanley Market** (p35) and the waterfront bars and restaurants; there's an OK **beach** to the south-east where you can rent windsurfers. At the western end of the bay is historic **Murray House** (see the boxed text below), moved brick by brick from Central and now containing a couple of restaurants.

At the western end of Stanley's Main St, past a tiny shrine devoted to Tai Wong and through the modern shopping complex called Stanley Plaza, is **Tin Hau Temple** (☎ 2813 0418; 119 Stanley Main St; ☾ 7am-5.30pm), built in 1767 and said to be the oldest building still standing in Hong Kong. It has undergone a complete renovation since then, but the interior remains traditional. If you follow the path behind the temple and continue up the hill, you'll reach the **Kwun Yam Temple** (☎ 2813 1849; ☾ 7am-6pm).

INFORMATION
15km south of Central
🚌 6, 6A, 6X, 260 (from Exchange Sq)
🍴 Lucy's (p76), Boathouse (p75)

Murray House (1846) – the world's largest jigsaw

Chinese Puzzle

When the Hong Kong government pulled down Hong Kong's oldest colonial building in 1982 to make room for the new Bank of China, it promised to rebuild Murray House elsewhere at a later date. The time came in the mid-1990s and the place chosen was Stanley – but the pieces had been so badly numbered and catalogued that it took workers 3½ years to put this colossal puzzle back together again. And, when they'd finished, they had six extra columns they didn't know what to do with.

Lamma Island (2, A3)

The third-largest island after Lantau and Hong Kong, Lamma is known for its seafood restaurants, beaches and hikes. The laid-back lifestyle, strong feeling of community and relatively low rental make it a popular place to live for expats.

Walking between the two main villages, **Yung Shue Wan** and **Sok Kwu Wan**, via popular **Hung Shing Yeh Beach** takes just over an hour. South of the beach, the path climbs steeply until it reaches a pavilion near the top of the hill. This is a nice place to relax, despite the clear view of the power station to the north. Further on you'll come to a ridge where you can look down on Sok Kwu Wan, a small place supporting a dozen or so waterfront seafood restaurants.

> **INFORMATION**
> *10km south of Central*
> 🚢 Central (outlying islands ferry terminal, pier 4) to Yung Shue Wan or Sok Kwu Wan; Aberdeen to Yung Shue Wan or Sok Kwu Wan
> 💲 Yung Shue Wan & Sok Kwu Wan to Central ($10-20), to Aberdeen ($8-12)
> ℹ️ Hong Kong & Kowloon Ferry (☎ 2815 6063; www.hkkf.com.hk); Chuen Kee Ferry (☎ 2375 7883; www.ferry.com.hk)
> ✖️ Bookworm Café, 79 Main St, Yung Shue Wan (vegetarian); Rainbow Restaurant, Shops 1A-1B, 23-24 First St, Sok Kwu Wan (seafood)

Sai Kung (1, D1)

Apart from the Outlying Islands, the Sai Kung Peninsula is one of the last havens left in Hong Kong for hikers, swimmers and boaters, and most of it is one huge 7600-hectare country park.

A short journey to any of the islands off Sai Kung town is rewarding. Hidden away are some excellent beaches that can be visited by *kaido* (small boat), which depart from the waterfront. Most head over to **Sharp Island** (Kiu Tsui Chau) about 1.5km away. Both **Hap Mun**, a sandy beach to the south, and **Kiu Tsu**, a beach on the western shore, can be reached by *kaido*. **Sai Kung town** boasts some excellent seafood restaurants along its waterfront.

The **MacLehose Trail**, a 100km route across the New Territories, begins at **Pak Tam Chung** (1, D1) on the Sai Kung Peninsula. The first couple of stages follow the perimeter of High Island Reservoir and offer fantastic coastal views.

> **INFORMATION**
> *25km northeast of Central*
> 🚌 94 from Sai Kung town to Sai Kung East Country Park & Pak Tam Chung (MacLehose Trail stage No 1)
> Ⓜ Choi Hung then 🚌 minibus 1A & 1M or 🚌 92
> 🚆 Sha Tin KCR East Rail then 🚌 299
> ℹ️ Country & Marine Parks Authority (☎ 2420 0529; http://parks.afcd.gov.hk)
> ✖️ Tung Kee (☎ 2792 7453; 96-102 Man Nin St; 🕐 6am-11pm)

Macau (1, A3)

Only an hour's boat ride to the west of Hong Kong, this charming fusion of Asian and Mediterranean cultures makes a magnificent getaway. Returned to Chinese sovereignty in 1999 after four-and-a-half centuries under Portuguese rule, Macau is now a Special Administrative Region of China.

The tiny (27.3 sq km) territory consists of the Macau Peninsula, which is attached to China, and the islands Taipa and Coloane, connected by bridges to the mainland and by landfill to each other. About 95% of the population is Chinese and most visitors are gamblers drawn to the casinos, but Macau boasts some picture-postcard churches and civil buildings, narrow streets, traditional shops and Portuguese and Macanese restaurants, all of which make it well worth a visit.

INFORMATION

65km west of Central

- 🚢 Macau ferry pier in Sheung Wan; China ferry terminal in Tsim Sha Tsui
- 💲 ferry $140-175 (Hong Kong dollars are accepted across Macau; beware: local patacas are all but impossible to exchange outside Macau)
- ℹ️ Macau Government Tourist Office (☎ 853-315 566, 397 1120; www.macautourism .gov.mo; 9 Largo do Senado; ⏰ 9am-6pm); ferry terminal branch (☎ 853-726 416; ⏰ 9am-10pm) You need your passport to visit Macau; Central Macau is best explored on foot, and taxis are cheap for attractions further afield.
- 🍴 A Lorcha (☎ 853-313 193; 289a Rua do Almirante Sérgio) This much-loved Portuguese restaurant faces the Inner Harbour northwest of Macau Tower; book ahead.

Largo do Senado

'Senate Square', with its wavy black-and-white cobbles and beautiful colonial buildings, is the heart and soul of Macau; the square and its buildings are illuminated at night. Lovely Santa Casa da Misericordia (☎ 853-573 938; Travessa da Misericordia 2; admission $5; ⏰ 10-1pm & 3-5.30pm Mon-Sat), on the southern side of the square, was a home for orphans and prostitutes in the 18th century. ✉️ **Avenida de Almeida Ribeiro (opposite Leal Senado)**

Leal Senado

Macau's most important historical building, the 'Loyal Senate' now houses the mayor's office, an art gallery and the ornately furnished Senate Library. Above the entrance to the peaceful courtyard garden is a heraldic inscription dating from 1654 that refers to Macau's support during Spain's 60-year occupation of Portugal. ☎ 853-387 333 ✉️ 163 **Avenida de Almeida**

Largo do Senado illuminated at night

Ribeiro $ free
🗓 gallery 9am-9pm
Tue-Sun, library 1-7pm
Mon-Sat

Ruins of the Church of St Paul

The façade and majestic stairway are all that remain of this church designed by an Italian Jesuit and built by Japanese Christian exiles in the early 1600s. However, with its wonderful statues, portals and engravings, some consider it to be the greatest monument to Christianity in Asia.
✉ **Rua de São Paulo**

Macau Museum

Housed in 17th-century Monte Fort, this wonderful museum tells the story of the hybrid territory of Macau, with a host of multimedia exhibits focusing on its history, traditions and culture.
☎ 853-357 911
✉ **Praceta do Museum de Macau, Fortaleza do Monte** $ $15/8, free on 15th of each month
🗓 10am-6pm Tue-Sun

Macau Tower

At 338m, this is the 10th-tallest free-standing tower in the world. The views across Macau's islands and city centre from the observation decks are spectacular, and the myriad climbs and walks on offer here cause much horror and hilarity.

☎ 853-988 8858
🖥 www.macautower.com.mo ✉ **Largo da Torre de Macau**
$ observation decks $70/35, climbs & walks from $100 🗓 10am-9pm Mon-Fri, 9am-9pm Sat & Sun

Lou Lim Loc Garden

This wonderful garden has huge shade trees, lotus ponds, bamboo groves, grottoes and a bridge with nine turns to escape from evil spirits (who can only move in straight lines). Local people use the park to practise t'ai chi or play traditional Chinese musical instruments.
✉ **10 Estrada de Adolfo de Loureiro** $ free
🗓 6am-9pm

Church of St Dominic

Arguably the most beautiful in Macau, this 17th-century baroque church contains the Treasury of Sacred Art (☎ 853-367 706; admission free; 🗓 10am-6pm), an Aladdin's Cave of ecclesiastical art and liturgical plates.
✉ **Largo de São Domingos** $ free 🗓 8am-5pm

Kun Iam Statue

Though it sounds naff, this 20m-high bronze monument to the goddess of mercy emerging from a lotus is a sublime harbourside sight. Beneath the statue is the Kun Iam Ecumenical Centre (☎ 853-751 516), a fine place for contemplation.
✉ **Avenida Doutor Sun Yat Sen** $ free 🗓 10am-6pm Sat-Thu

Lou Lim Loc Garden – evil spirits need not apply

ORGANISED TOURS

Tourism is one of Hong Kong's biggest money-spinners, so it's no surprise that there is a mind-boggling array of tours available via every conceivable conveyance. Some of the best tours are offered by the **Hong Kong Tourism Board** (HKTB; ☎ 2508 1234; www.discoverhongkong .com), and tours run by individual companies can usually be booked at any HKTB branch (p119).

The HKTB invites visitors on a free ride on a sailing junk on Thursday. Boarding is at 3pm and 5pm at Queen's Pier (4, D3) in Central and the public pier next to the Star Ferry Terminal (3, B9) in Tsim Sha Tsui, but visitors should register with any HKTB branch in advance.

Boat Tours

Aberdeen & Harbour Night Cruise

This four- to five-hour cruise to Aberdeen on a junk includes unlimited drinks and a seafood dinner at a floating restaurant. After dinner you're taken by coach to Stubbs Rd Lookout for a view of Hong Kong by night.
☎ 2926 3868 🖳 http://webserv1.discoverhongkong.com/eng/touring/night/ta_nigh_138812.jhtml 💲 $660/540 ⏱ hotel pick-up from 5.15pm

Dolphinwatch

As well as a scenic dolphin-spotting expedition, the four-hour tour off Lantau Island offered by Dolphinwatch includes information on the plight of the endangered Chinese white dolphin and Hong Kong's precarious environmental situation. Between 100 and 200 of these mammals inhabit Hong Kong's coastal waters.
☎ 2984 1414 🖳 www.hkdolphinwatch.com 💲 $320/160 ⏱ 8.30 or 9am-1 or 1.30pm

Sai Kung Powerboat Trips

NEI's fabulous five-hour tour of the harbour around Sai Kung takes you by unique 'fast-pursuit craft' to the otherwise inaccessible Bluff Island and the small fishing village of Sha Kiu Tau. The tour price includes seafood lunch and all gear, including mask and snorkel. See the website for other tour details.
☎ 2486 2112 🖳 www.kayak-and-hike.com 💲 $595 ⏱ 9am Tue & Thu

Food ahoy!

Sea & Land Tour

These full-day Sea & Land tours (seven to eight hours) run by Splendid Tours & Travel take you out on the harbour by boat in the morning and offer you one of two coach tours in the afternoon: a Hong Kong Island orientation tour or one of Kowloon and the New Territories. Price includes dim sum lunch.

☎ 2316 2151 ⌨ www .splendidtours.com 💲 $480/390 ⏰ 10.15 or 10.30am

Bus Tours

Deluxe Hong Kong Island Tour

Gray Line, the stalwart tour company, has two daily, five-hour tours that take in Man Mo Temple, Victoria Peak, Aberdeen, Repulse

---

Cultural Kaleidoscope

Another one of the superb HKTB offerings is a series of free cultural programs in English called 'Meet the People' run by local experts in their fields. For times, days and venues, contact the Hong Kong Tourist Board (HKTB; ☎ 2508 1234; www.discoverhong kong.com).

- Antiques Appreciation Class
- Architecture Walk
- Cantonese Opera Appreciation Class
- Feng Shui Class
- Kung Fu Corner Demonstration & Class
- Secrets of Jade Shopping
- Secrets of Pearl Shopping
- T'ai Chi Class

Bay and Stanley, including the market.

☎ 2368 7111 ⌨ www .grayline.com.hk 💲 $295/190 ⏰ hotel pick-up 7.50-9am & 1-2.30pm

Suss out the city's shopping secrets

The Land Between

This 6½-hour New Territories tour operated by Gray Line takes you to places that could be a hassle to get to independently, such as the Yuen Yuen Institute temple complex in Tsuen Wan, the Tai Mo Shan lookout and the Sam Mun Tsai fishing village. The tour price includes lunch.

☎ 2368 7111 ⌨ www .grayline.com.hk 💲 $395/345 ⏰ hotel pick-up 8.30-9am & 1-1.30pm

Lantau Explorer Bus

The Lantau Explorer Pass includes return ferry transportation between Central and Mui Wo and a bus tour of Lantau, with three stops: Cheung Sha Beach (15 minutes), Ngong Ping and Tian Tan Buddha (two hours), and Tai O village (one hour).

☎ 2984 8255 💲 $150 ⏰ 10.30am (ferry) & 11.45 (bus) Mon-Sat, 10.30am (ferry) & noon (bus) Sun

Shopping

Shopping in Hong Kong is not just about buying stuff: it's a social activity, a form of recreation, a way of life for many people, both locals and expatriates. Though it isn't the bargain basement it once was, Hong Kong still wins for variety and its passionate embrace of competitive consumerism. Any international brand worthy of its logo sets up at least one shop here, and there are a slew of local brands worth spending your money on. Clothing (ready-made or tailored), shoes, jewellery, luggage and, to lesser a degree nowadays, electronic goods are the city's strong suits.

There are no sales taxes so the marked price is the price you'll pay. Credit cards are widely accepted, except in markets. It's rare for traders to accept travellers cheques or foreign currency as payment. Sales assistants in department or chain stores rarely have any leeway to give discounts, but you can try bargaining in owner-operated shops and certainly in markets.

You can count on shops in Central to be open from 10am to between 6pm and 7.30pm daily. In Causeway Bay and Wan Chai, many will stay open until 9.30pm or 10pm. In Tsim Sha Tsui, Yau Ma Tei and Mong Kok, they close around 9pm.

Shopping Areas

Main shopping areas are Central (4) and Causeway Bay (5) on Hong Kong Island and Tsim Sha Tsui (3) in Kowloon. Nathan Rd in Tsim Sha Tsui is the main tourist strip, and one of very few places where you'll find merchants poised to rip you off, especially when buying electronic goods or photographic equipment. Central has a mix of mid-range to top-end street-front retail and shopping malls; it's a good area to look for things like cameras, books, antiques and designer threads. Causeway Bay is a crush of department stores and smaller outlets selling eclectic fashion. For market shopping see p35.

Well, 'eclectic fashion' is one way of putting it...

Defensive Shopping

Most shops are loath to give refunds but they can usually be persuaded to exchange purchases that can be resold; just make sure you get a detailed receipt. When buying electronic goods, always beware of merchandise imported by an unauthorised agent, as this may void your warranty.

If you have any trouble with dodgy merchants, contact the Quality Tourism Services (QTS) scheme of the **HKTB** (☎ 2806 2823; www.qtshk.com) if they are members of that association (the HKTB logo should be displayed on the front door if so). Otherwise, call the **Hong Kong Consumer Council** (☎ 2929 2222; www .consumer.org.hk).

ANTIQUES & FURNISHINGS

Hong Kong has a rich array of Asian antiques and curios for sale, but serious collectors will restrict themselves to the reputable shops and auction houses. This is an area where the uninitiated can easily be fooled (and sometimes seriously burned).

Arch Angel Antiques (6, A2)
Though the specialities are antique and ancient porcelain and tomb ware, Arch Angel packs a lot more into its three floors: there's everything from mah jong sets and terracotta horses to palatial furniture. You'll feel as comfortable here buying a small gift as a feature ornament for the salon.
☎ 2851 6828 ⊠ 53-55 Hollywood Rd, Central 🕑 9.30am-6.30pm 🚌 26 Ⓜ Central, Sheung Wan

Chine Gallery (6, A2)
Sells carefully restored furniture (we love the lacquered cabinets) from all over China and hand-knotted rugs from remote regions such as Xinjiang, Ningxia, Gansu, Inner Mongolia and Tibet.
☎ 2543 0023 🖳 www.chinegallery.com ⊠ 42a Hollywood Rd, Central 🕑 10am-6pm Mon-Sat, 1-6pm Sun 🚌 26 Ⓜ Central, Sheung Wan

Hobbs & Bishops Fine Art (6, B2)
This shop smelling of bees wax specialises in lacquered Chinese wooden furniture from the 19th and early 20th centuries. Their eye tends more to sleekly handsome than ostentatious pieces.
☎ 2537 9838 ⊠ 28 Hollywood Rd, Central 🕑 10am-5.30pm Mon-Sat 🚌 26 Ⓜ Central, Sheung Wan

Karin Weber Antiques (6, A1)
Karin Weber has a good mix of Chinese country antiques and contemporary Asian artworks. She gives short lectures on antiques and the scene in Hong Kong and provides shopping services into Guangdong for serious buyers.
☎ 2544 5004 🖳 www.karinwebergallery.com ⊠ 20 Aberdeen St, Soho 🕑 11am-7pm Mon-Sat Ⓜ Central, Sheung Wan 🚌 26

Tai Sing Fine Antiques (6, C3)
Tai Sing has been selling quality Chinese antiques for 50 years with a special focus on porcelain. Two of the shop's six floors are now devoted to European furniture, including a great assembly of Art Deco pieces.
☎ 2525 9365 ⊠ 12 Wyndham St, Central 🕑 10am-6pm Mon-Sat Ⓜ Central

Tibetan Gallery (6, B2)
This small shop has an impressive selection of Tibetan religious art and artefacts, including mini-altars. There's a showroom on the 1st floor.
☎ 2530 4863 ⊠ Ground & 1st fl, Yu Yuet Lai Bldg, 55 Wyndham St, Central 🕑 10.30am-7.30pm Mon-Sat, noon-6pm Sun 🚌 26 Ⓜ Central

Shipping News
Goods can be sent home by post, and some shops will package and post the goods for you. It's a good idea to find out whether you will have to clear the goods at the other end. If the goods are fragile, it is sensible to buy 'all risks' insurance.

Smaller items can be shipped from the post office. **United Parcel Service** (UPS; ☎ 2735 3535) also offers services from Hong Kong to some 40 countries. It ships by air and accepts parcels weighing up to 30kg. **DHL** (☎ 2400 3388) is another option.

BOOKS

Hong Kong now counts more bookshops than ever before and most are on Hong Kong Island.

Bookazine (4, C3)

This chain operates atmosphere-free store branches all around Hong Kong. Each shop stocks a dependable range of books, magazines and stationery.
☎ 2521 1649 ✉ Ground fl, Pacific House, 20 Queen's Rd Central
🕙 9.30am-7.30pm Mon-Sat, 10am-6.30pm
Ⓜ Central 🚻 Yes

Cosmos Books (4, G5)

This outlet has a good selection of Chinese-related books in the basement. Upstairs there are English-language books (nonfiction is quite strong) plus one of the city's best stationery departments.
☎ 2866 1677 ✉ Basement & 1st fl, 30 Johnston Rd, Wan Chai 🕙 10am-8pm Ⓜ Central 🚻 Yes

Dymocks (4, D3)

Australia's Dymocks chain offers a solid mainstream selection of page-turners, travel books and magazines. There's a smaller branch in Central's Star Ferry concourse (4, D3).
☎ 2117 0360 💻 www.dymocks.com.hk ✉ Shop 2007-2011, 2nd fl, IFC Mall, 1 Harbour View St, Central
🕙 8.30am-9.30pm Mon-Sat, 9am-9pm Sun
Ⓜ Central

Flow Bookshop (6, B2)

This exchange/second-hand bookshop has a focus on spiritual literature.
☎ 2964 9483 ✉ 1st fl,

Lyndhurst Tce, Central (enter from Cochrane St)
🕙 noon-7pm Ⓜ Central

Government Publications Office (4, D4)

This is the place to come for hiking maps of Hong Kong's hills and country parks.
☎ 2537 1910 ✉ Rm 402, 4th fl, Murray Bldg, 22 Garden Rd, Central
🕙 9am-6pm Mon-Fri, 9am-noon Sat Ⓜ Central

Hong Kong Book Centre (4, C3)

This basement shop has a vast selection of books and magazines, including a mammoth number of business titles.
☎ 2522 7064 💻 www.swindonbooks.com ✉ Basement, On Lok Yuen Bldg, 25 Des Voeux

Rd Central 🕙 9am-6.30pm Mon-Fri, 9am-5.30pm Sat, 1-5pm Sun (summer only) Ⓜ Central 🚻 Yes

Joint Publishing Company (6, C1)

Joint, with some 17 branches scattered throughout the territory, is outstanding for books about China and studying Chinese languages. Most English titles, including the patchy but creditable literature section, are on the mezzanine.
☎ 2868 6844 ✉ 9 Queen Victoria St, Central
🕙 10.30am-7.30pm Mon-Sat, 1-6pm Sun
Ⓜ Central 🚻 Yes

Kelly & Walsh (4, E4)

This is a smart shop with a good selection of art, design

and culinary books. The children's books are shelved in a handy kids' reading lounge.
☎ 2522 5743 ✉ Shop 236, 2nd fl, Pacific Place, 88 Queensway, Admiralty ◷ 10.30am-8pm Sun-Thu, 10.30am-8.30pm Fri & Sat Ⓜ Admiralty 🚋 Yes

Page One (3, B7)
A chain, yes, but one with attitude. Page One has Hong Kong's best selection of art and design magazines and books; it's also strong on photography, literature, film and children's books.
☎ 2730 6080 ✉ Shop 3002, 3rd fl, Gateway Arcade, Harbour City, Canton Rd, Tsim Sha Tsui ◷ 10.30am-9pm ⛴ Star Ferry (Tsim Sha Tsui) Ⓜ Tsim Sha Tsui

Swindon Books (3, C8)
Swindon, behind the Hyatt Regency, is one of the larger, more established booksellers. Its sister store is the Hong Kong Book Centre.
☎ 2366 8001 🖥 www .swindonbooks.com ✉ 13-15 Lock Rd, Tsim Sha Tsui ◷ 9am-6.30pm Mon-Thu, 9am-7.30pm Fri & Sat, 12.30-6.30pm Sun Ⓜ Tsim Sha Tsui

Tai Yip Art Book Centre (6, B2)
Tai Yip has a terrific selection of books about anything Chinese and artsy: calligraphy, jade, bronze, costumes, architecture, symbolism. This art book centre also has branches at the Hong Kong Museum of Art (p26) and the Hong Kong Museum of History (p13).
☎ 2524 5963 🖥 www .taiyipart.com.hk ✉ Room 101-102, 1st fl, Capitol Plaza, 2-10 Lyndhurst Tce, Central ◷ 10am-9pm Mon-Fri, 10am-6.30pm Sat & Sun Ⓜ Central

CARPETS

While carpets aren't really that cheap, there's a good selection of silk and wool (new and antique) carpets in several areas, especially in Central.

Caravan (6, A1)
A shop called Caravan with an owner named Driver? Trustworthy rug-sellers travel all over Asia to stock this nicely cluttered shop. The range of Afghan and Tibetan carpets is especially notable.
☎ 2547 3821 ✉ 65 Hollywood Rd, Central ◷ 10am-7pm 🚌 26 Ⓜ Central, Sheung Wan

Chinese Carpet Centre Ltd (3, D9)
You'll be floored by the huge selection of new carpets and rugs here; most of them are made in China and many of them are 100% silk.
☎ 2736 1773 ✉ Shop L021, Ground fl, New World Centre, Salisbury Rd, Tsim Sha Tsui ◷ 10am-7pm Ⓜ Tsim Sha Tsui

Mir Oriental Carpets (6, B3)
One of Hong Kong's largest stockists of fine rugs, with thousands of carpets from around the world flying in and out of the shop. The modern Persian carpets are out of this world.
☎ 2521 5641 ✉ Ground fl, New India House, 52 Wyndham St ◷ 10am-6.30pm Mon-Sat, 11am-5pm Sun 🚌 26 Ⓜ Central

Top-of-the-line teddy bears in action

CHILDREN'S ITEMS

There's a surprising dearth of shops devoted to babies and children, but the ones that do exist are stocked with quality clothing and toys.

Toto (4, D3)
Jumpsuits and other togs for under-twos; everything made by this Hong Kong brand is 100% cotton.
☎ 2869 4668 🖥 www .totobaby.com ✉ Shop 212, 2nd fl, Prince's Bldg, 10 Chater Rd, Central ✆ 10am-6.30pm Mon-Sat Ⓜ Central ⓦ Yes

Toy Museum (4, D3)
Top-of-the-line teddy bears, action men, beanie babies

and Pokemon paraphernalia. There's a great collection of old GI Joes for dads to amuse themselves with, and a toy hospital too.
☎ 2869 9138 ✉ Shop 320, 3rd fl, Prince's Bldg, 10 Chater Rd, Central ✆ 10am-7pm Mon-Sat, noon-5.30pm Sun Ⓜ Central ⓦ Yes

Wise Kids (4, E4)
Nothing to plug in and nothing with batteries:

Wise Kids concentrates on kids generating energy with what's upstairs. Along with stuffed toys, card games and things to build, there are practical items for parents such as toilet-lid locks and carry-alls.
☎ 2868 0133 🖥 www .wisekidstoys.com ✉ Shop 134, 1st fl, Pacific Place, 88 Queensway, Admiralty ✆ 10am-8pm Sun-Wed, 10am-9pm Thu-Sat Ⓜ Admiralty ⓦ Yes

CLOTHING & ACCESSORIES

The best hunting grounds for warehouse sales and factory extras are generally in Tsim Sha Tsui at the eastern end of Granville Rd (3, D7). Also check out nearby Austin Ave (3, D6) and Chatham Rd South (3, D7).

Jardine's Bazaar (5, B4) in Causeway Bay has low-cost garments, and there are several sample shops for cheap jeans in Lee Garden Rd (5, B4). The street markets (p35) in Yau Ma Tei and Mong Kok have the cheapest clothes. Also try Li Yuen St East and West (4, C3), two narrow alleyways linking Des Voeux Rd Central with Queen's Rd Central, which are a jumble of inexpensive clothing, handbags and jewellery. For mid-priced items, Causeway Bay and Tsim Sha Tsui, particularly east of Nathan Rd (3, C9), are good hunting grounds.

Blanc De Chine (4, C3)
A sumptuous shop that specialises in men's traditional Chinese jackets, off the rack or made to measure. For women there's a lovely selection of silk dresses.
☎ 2524 7875 ✉ Shop 201-203A, 2nd fl, Pedder Bldg, 12 Pedder St, Central ✆ 10am-7pm Ⓜ Central ⓦ Yes

Dada Cabaret Voltaire (5, B4)
Ragged rainbow colours

that are also sported by the staff. Just one of many fine shops in the Fashion Island micro mall complex.
☎ 2890 1708 ✉ Shop F-13A, 1st fl, Fashion Island, 19 Great George St, Causeway Bay ✆ noon-10pm Ⓜ Causeway Bay ⓦ Yes

i.t Shop (3, C7)
This shop and the women's-only b+ab shop next door both sell the cute, trendy gear that can be found everywhere in Hong Kong.

There are i.t shops in all the major shopping areas.
☎ 2736 9152 ✉ Shop 1030, Miramar Shopping Centre, 1-23 Kimberley Rd, Tsim Sha Tsui ✆ noon-10pm Ⓜ Tsim Sha Tsui

Joyce Ma (4, C4)
This multi-designer store (and Hong Kong institution) is a good choice if you're pressed for time, with Issey Miyake, Yves Saint Laurent, Jean Paul Gaultier, Commes

des Garçons, Voyage, Yohji Yamamoto and some Hong Kong fashion all on display. There's also a branch at Pacific Place (4, E4).
☎ 2810 1120 🖳 www .joyce.com ✉ Ground fl, New World Tower, 16 Queen's Rd Central ✠ 10.30am-7.30pm Mon-Sat, 11am-7pm Sun Ⓜ Central ♿ Yes

Kent & Curwen (4, E4)
Distinguished suits, dress shirts, ties, cufflinks and casual tops for the gentleman who'd rather look to the manor born than dotcom upstart.
☎ 2840 0023 ✉ Shop 372, 3rd fl, Pacific Place, 88 Queensway, Admiralty ✠ 10am-7.30pm Ⓜ Admiralty ♿ Yes

Lids (3, D7)
The coolest headgear – from baseball caps begging to be turned back to front to helmets for cyclists, rollerbladers and skateboarders.
☎ 2366 1371 🖳 www .lids.com ✉ Shop 2, Park

Hotel, 61-65 Chatham Rd Sth, Tsim Sha Tsui ✠ 11am-11pm Ⓜ Tsim Sha Tsui

Miu Miu (4, C3)
Super-cute and creative threads for neo-adults are available here. The shoes are exceptionally stylish.
☎ 2523 7833 ✉ Shop B24, Basement 1, Landmark, 1 Pedder St, Central ✠ 10.30am-7.30pm Mon-Sat, 11am-7pm Sun Ⓜ Central ♿ Yes

Shanghai Tang (4, C3)
This stylish shop has sparked something of a fashion wave in Hong Kong with its updated versions of traditional yet neon-coloured Chinese garments. Shanghai Tang also has accessories and delightful gift items.
☎ 2525 7333 🖳 www .shanghaitang.com ✉ Basement & ground fl, Pedder Bldg, 12 Pedder St, Central ✠ 10am-8pm Mon-Sat, noon-6m Sun Ⓜ Central ♿ Yes

Spy (5, A4)
Tame yet trendy everyday wear such as slacks and short-sleeve shirts from designer Henry Lau.
☎ 2893 7799, 2317 6928 🖳 www.spyhenrylau .com ✉ Shop C, Ground fl, 11 Sharp St East, Causeway Bay ✠ 1-11pm Ⓜ Causeway Bay

Travelmax (3, A9)
Outdoor gear for all seasons, including sizes for kids. There's a good range of Eagle Creek travel products here too.
☎ 3188 4271 ✉ Shop 270-273, 2nd fl, Ocean Terminal, Harbour City, Canton Rd, Tsim Sha Tsui ✠ 10am-9pm ⛴ Star Ferry (Tsim Sha Tsui) Ⓜ Tsim Sha Tsui

Vivienne Tam (4, E4)
Sophisticated yet adventurous women's wear from New York–based designer Vivienne Tam, who was trained in Hong Kong.
☎ 2918 0238 🖳 www .viviennetam.com

CLOTHING & SHOE SIZES

Women's Clothing

Aust/UK	8	10	12	14	16	18
Europe	36	38	40	42	44	46
Japan	5	7	9	11	13	15
USA	6	8	10	12	14	16

Women's Shoes

Aust/USA	5	6	7	8	9	10
Europe	35	36	37	38	39	40
France only	35	36	38	39	40	42
Japan	22	23	24	25	26	27
UK	3½	4½	5½	6½	7½	8½

Men's Clothing

Aust	92	96	100	104	108	112
Europe	46	48	50	52	54	56

Japan	S	M	M		L	
UK/USA	35	36	37	38	39	40

Men's Shirts (Collar Sizes)

Aust/Japan	38	39	40	41	42	43
Europe	38	39	40	41	42	43
UK/USA	15	15½	16	16½	17	17½

Men's Shoes

Aust/UK	7	8	9	10	11	12
Europe	41	42	43	44½	46	47
Japan	26	27	27.5	28	29	30
USA	7½	8½	9½	10½	11½	12½

Measurements approximate only; try before you buy.

✉ **Shop 209, 2nd fl, Pacific Place, 88 Queensway, Admiralty** ⏰ 11am-8pm Sun-Thu, 11am-9pm Fri & Sat Ⓜ Admiralty 🚇 Yes

Wanko (4, C3)
Soft spring-colour skirts and blouses as well as sharper business attire on offer. Of course, some people shop here just for the name; 'I bought it at Wanko' does have a certain ring to it. ☎ 2523 0520 ✉ **Shop 209, Ground fl, Chinese Bank Bldg, 31-37 Des Voeux Rd Central** ⏰ 11am-9.30pm Ⓜ Central 🚇 Yes

www.izzue.com (3, B8)
You'll find simple, energetic and comfortable styles in this chain of super-groovy boutiques. There are a dozen other outlets throughout the territory, including a Central branch (4, C4). ☎ 2992 0631 🖥 www.izzue.com ✉ **Shop 2225, 2nd fl, Gateway Arcade, Harbour City, Canton Rd, Tsim Sha Tsui** ⏰ 11am-9pm 🚢 Star Ferry (Tsim Sha Tsui) Ⓜ Tsim Sha Tsui

Sale On

Winter sales are during the first three weeks of January and summer sales are in late June and early July. In mid-July Hong Kong pretties itself up for Fashion Week, the industry's most important annual event. The main parades and events take place at the Hong Kong Convention and Exhibition Centre (7, B1) in Wan Chai, but keep an eye out for well-dressed shindigs in shopping centres around the territory.

COMPUTERS & ELECTRONIC GOODS

Hong Kong is a popular place to buy computers, but while prices are competitive, be careful what you buy and where you buy it from and make sure you get an international warranty with your computer.

1010 (3, B7)
The latest, smallest, sleekest in mobile phones and palm pilots – pure binary finery. There's a branch at Century Square (6, C2) in Central. ☎ 2910 1010 🖥 www.hkcsl.com ✉ 82-84 Canton Rd, Tsim Sha Tsui ⏰ 10am-11pm Ⓜ Tsim Sha Tsui

Mong Kok Computer Centre (3, C1)
Three floors of computer shops. Though geared more towards the Cantonese-speaking market than the foreign one, you can generally get better deals than in Tsim Sha Tsui. Check Winframe System (☎ 2300 1238; Shop 106-107, 1st fl) or Fortune Computer (☎ 2359 9018; Shop 221, 2nd fl). ☎ 2781 1109 ✉ 8-8a Nelson St, Mong Kok ⏰ 10am-9pm Ⓜ Mong Kok

Star Computer City (3, B9)
The largest complex of retail computer outlets in Tsim Sha Tsui, with some two dozen shops. Have a look at Reptron (☎ 2730 2891; Shop A1, 2nd fl) for desktops, laptops and PDAs, and 2C (☎ 2375 2375; Shop D1-2, 2nd fl) for accessories such as modem protectors, various adaptors and cables etc. ☎ 2736 2608 ✉ 2nd fl, Star House, 3 Salisbury Rd, Tsim Sha Tsui ⏰ 10 or 10.30am-7.30 or 8pm 🚢 Star Ferry (Tsim Sha Tsui) Ⓜ Tsim Sha Tsui

Circuitry Circus

Golden Plaza Shopping Centre (2, B1; 146-152 Fuk Wah St, Sham Shui Po), just opposite the Sham Shui Po MTR station, is the place for cheap software of somewhat dubious origin, games, and accessories like keyboards, printer cartridges, CDs and DVDs. Most shops open daily 10am to 10pm but some don't open until noon. It's packed at the weekend.

DEPARTMENT STORES

Hong Kong's department stores stock everything from clothing to groceries. However, if you're looking for bargains look elsewhere.

Lane Crawford (6, C2)
The original branch of Hong Kong's first Western-style department store. It's still an upscale place – a sort of local response to Harvey Nichols in London. There are branches at Pacific Place in Admiralty (4, E4), Times Square in Causeway Bay (5, A4) and Ocean Terminal in Tsim Sha Tsui (3, B9).
☎ 2118 3388 💻 www .lanecrawford.com ✉ 70 Queen's Rd Central 🕑 10am-9pm Ⓜ Central 🚻 Yes

Sogo (5, B4)
This Japanese-owned store at the hub of Causeway Bay has 13 well-organised floors and more than 37,000 sq metres of retail space. The range is

mind-boggling: over 20 brands of neckties just for starters. Eclectic departments include the 'baby train models' area and Beauté@Sogo.
☎ 2833 8338 💻 www .sogo.com.hk ✉ 555 Hennessy Rd, Causeway Bay 🕑 10am-10pm Ⓜ Causeway Bay 🚻 Yes

Wing On (4, B2)
This department store is notable for being locally owned. It carries the full range but is especially known for electronics and household appliances. There is also a Tsim Sha Tsui branch on Nathan Rd (3, C5).
☎ 2852 1888 ✉ 211 Des Voeux Rd Central 🕑 10am-7.30pm Ⓜ Sheung Wan 🚻 Yes

Multi-level shopping bliss

Yue Hwa (3, C5)
This cavernous place is everything a visiting souvenir-hunter could ask for – seven packed floors of ceramics, furniture, souvenirs and clothing, as well as bolts of silk, herbs, clothes, porcelain, luggage, umbrellas and kitchenware. It's the biggest and best of more than a dozen branches of Yue Hwa in Hong Kong.
☎ 2384 0084 💻 www .yuehwa.com ✉ 301-309 Nathan Rd, Yau Ma Tei 🕑 10am-10pm Ⓜ Jordan

---

Hong Kong Stitch-Up
Need a tailor? Take a walk on Nathan Rd and they'll find you, or ask your hotel concierge. Otherwise, try **Pacific Custom Tailors** (4, E4; ☎ 2845 5377; Shop 110, 1st fl, Pacific Place, 88 Queensway, Admiralty) or **Sam's Tailor** (3, C7; ☎ 2367 9423; Shop K, Burlington Arcade, 92-94 Nathan Rd, Tsim Sha Tsui). The turnaround is about 48 hours, including two fittings.

FOOD, DRINK & SMOKES

In a city that places so much importance on things culinary, you're bound to find some interesting shops with edible (and drinkable) specialities.

Cigarro (4, D3)
Sometimes you do need a fat cigar to feel like you're making it big in the big city. This place comes to the res-

cue with Cuban, Dominican and other fine stogies.
☎ 2810 1883 💻 www .clubalegria.com ✉ Shop 5, Ground fl, St George's

Bldg, 2 Ice House St, Central 🕑 10am-9pm Mon-Fri, 10am-8pm Sat, noon-6pm Sun Ⓜ Central 🚻 Yes

city'super (4, D2)

Gourmet supermarket with ready-to-eats such as sushi and salads and fresh produce that has been flown in at high prices. Even if you're not in the market, it's worth a browse. There's a branch at Gateway Arcade, Harbour City, Tsim Sha Tsui (3, B7). ☎ 2234 7128 ⌨ www .citysuper.com.hk ✉ Shop 1041-1049, 1st fl, IFC Mall, 1 Harbour View St, Central ⏰ 10.30am-9.30pm Ⓜ Central

Fook Ming Tong Tea Shop (4, C3)

Teas of various ages and propensities – from gunpowder ($8 for 37.55g) to Nanyan Ti Guan Yin Crown Grade ($780 for 150g) – and all sorts of tea-making accoutrements. Other shops include one in Ocean Terminal, Tsim Sha Tsui (3, A9). ☎ 2521 0337 ⌨ www .fookmingtong.com ✉ Shop G3-4, Ground fl, Landmark, 1 Pedder St, Central ⏰ 10am-7.30pm Mon-Sat, 11am-6pm Sun Ⓜ Central

Lock Cha Tea Shop (4, A2)

This is our favourite shop (enter from Ladder St) for Chinese teas, tea sets, wooden tea-boxes and well-presented gift packs of various cuppas. You can try before you buy. ☎ 2805 1360 ✉ 290b Queen's Rd Central, Sheung Wan ⏰ 11am-7pm Ⓜ Sheung Wan 🚌 26

Minamoto Kitchoan (3, C7)

These folk go to unbelievable lengths to make sweets so artistic that merely popping them into your mouth seems crude. Do it anyway and make it the *tosenka* (a big peach whose stone is replaced by a baby green peach) or *reika* (Japanese jelly flavoured with plum wine). ☎ 2368 6582 ⌨ www .kitchoan.com ✉ Shop G1, Ground fl, Tung Ying Bldg, 100 Nathan Rd, Tsim Sha Tsui ⏰ 11am-7pm Ⓜ Tsim Sha Tsui

Oliver's (4, D3)

The wood-panelled floors set the tone: this ain't no ordinary supermarket. Matzos or Mexican hot sauce? Got it. There's also a great range of international beers, the imported fruit and veggies obviously travel first class and the delicatessen stocks a wide range of cheeses, sausages, pâtés and fine wines. ☎ 2810 7710 ✉ Shop 201-205, Prince's Bldg, 10 Chater Rd, Central ⏰ 9am-8pm Ⓜ Central 🍴 Yes

Ponti Food & Wine Cellar (3, C8)

This wine shop stocks a huge range of table and vintage wines and holds attractive bin-end sales. There's a branch in Alexandra House, Central (4, D3). ☎ 2721 8770 ✉ Shop 3, Ground fl, Hong Kong Pacific Centre, 28 Hankow Rd, Tsim Sha Tsui ⏰ 11am-8.30pm Mon-Sat, 11am-8pm Sun Ⓜ Tsim Shi Tsui

---

Mall Trawl

Hong Kong is mall-rat heaven, but don't feel compelled to visit more than a couple: the same brands turn up over and over again.

Festival Walk (2, B1; 80-88 Tat Chee Ave, Kowloon Tong) A huge centre with a good mid-range selection of shops and restaurants, and an ice-skating rink.

Harbour City (3, B8; Canton Rd, Tsim Sha Tsui) The biggest mall with 700 shops in four separate zones.

IFC Mall (4, D2; 1 Harbour View St, Central) A bright, harbour-front centre with high-fashion boutiques, great restaurants and the airport railway terminal.

Landmark (4, C3; 1 Pedder St, Central) High fashion and good eating in a pleasant open space.

Pacific Place (4, E4; 88 Queensway, Admiralty) Piped jazz, free telephones and the classiest range of shops in town.

Prince's Building (4, D3; 10 Chater Rd, Central) Poky and disorienting but worth a look for its speciality fashion, and toy and kitchenware shops.

Times Square (5, A4; 1 Matheson St, Causeway Bay) A dozen floors organised by type: electronics (7th and 8th), a play area (9th) and food (10th to 13th).

JEWELLERY & COSMETICS

Jewellery exporting is big business in Hong Kong but don't expect any real bargains. Reputable jewellery shops will issue a certificate stating what you are buying and will guarantee to buy back at a fair market price.

Amours Antiques (6, A2)
This wonderful shop stocks rhinestone jewellery, frocks and a darling clutch of beaded and tapestry bags dating from the early 20th century. There's a branch in the Galleria, Central (4, F6).
☎ 2803 7877 ✉ 45 Staunton St, Soho
🕑 noon-8pm Mon-Sat
Ⓜ Central, Sheung Wan

J's (3, B8)
Affordable baubles for those who don't like ostentation. Most pieces are silver or white gold, some with small diamonds.
☎ 2736 8464 ✉ Shop 2522, 2nd fl, Gateway Arcade, Harbour City, Canton Rd, Tsim Sha Tsui
🕑 10.30am-8.30pm
🚢 Star Ferry (Tsim Sha Tsui) Ⓜ Tsim Sha Tsui

King Fook (4, C3)
Visit this fantastic-looking shop in the reputable King Fook jewellery chain just for its sheer garishness. There's also a wide range of watches and fountain pens. There's a branch in the Miramar Shopping Centre, Tsim Sha Tsui (3,C7).
☎ 2822 8573 🖥 www .kingfook.com ✉ 30-32 Des Voeux Rd Central
🕑 9.30am-7pm
Ⓜ Central 🈁 Yes

King Sing Jewellery (3, B9)
A long-established jewellers with a wide selection of

diamonds, pearls and gold items. The sales staff are pleasantly unpushy.
☎ 2735 7021 ✉ Shop 14, Ground fl, Star House, 3 Salisbury Rd, Tsim Sha Tsui 🕑 9.15am-7.30pm Mon-Sat, 9.15am-6.30pm Sun 🚢 Star Ferry (Tsim Sha Tsui) Ⓜ Tsim Sha Tsui

Om International (3, C8)
An excellent selection of saltwater and freshwater pearls, and a lot more on offer than what you see. The staff are honest and helpful.
☎ 2366 3421 ✉ 1st fl, Friend's House, 6 Carnarvon Rd, Tsim Sha Tsui 🕑 9.30am-6pm Mon-Sat Ⓜ Tsim Sha Tsui

Opal Mine (3, C7)
More of a museum than a shop, this place has a truly vast selection of Australian opals that makes for fascinating viewing and buying, should you be so tempted.
☎ 2721 9933 🖥 www .opalnet.com ✉ Shop G & H, Ground fl, Burlington Arcade, 92-94 Nathan Rd, Tsim Sha Tsui 🕑 9.30am-7pm Ⓜ Tsim Sha Tsui

Premier Jewellery (3, C8)
This third-generation family firm is directed by a qualified gemmologist and one of our favourite places to shop. The selection isn't huge but if you're looking for something particular, give them a day's notice to have a selection ready for your arrival. They can also help you design your own piece.
☎ 2368 0003 ✉ Shop G14-15, Ground fl, Holiday Inn Golden Mile Shopping Mall, 50 Nathan Rd, Tsim Sha Tsui 🕑 10am-7.30pm Mon-Sat, 10.30am-4pm Sun Ⓜ Tsim Sha Tsui

Shu Uemura (4, E4)
Visit this beauty boutique for your choice of mauve eyelashes, rust-coloured lipstick and skin-care advice, as well as a deluxe range of make-up brushes and soothing bath tonics. There's also a branch in the Landmark (4, C3), Central.
☎ 2918 1238 ✉ Shop 129, 1st fl, Pacific Place, 88 Queensway, Admiralty 🕑 10.30am-8.30pm Ⓜ Admiralty 🈁 Yes

Amazing what you find down alleyways

MUSIC

As well as the record shops listed below, the Temple St Night Market (p16) is the place to pick up cheap CDs, DVDs and video cassettes.

HMV (4, C3)
As long as you're not after anything too obscure, HMV will probably satisfy with its huge range of CDs, DVDs and magazines. There's also a branch located in Windsor House, Causeway Bay (5, B4). ☎ 2739 0268 ⌧ 1st fl, Central Bldg, 1-3 Pedder St, Central ☺ 9am-10pm Ⓜ Central 🚇 yes

Hong Kong Records (4, E4)
If you're looking for something different, this local outfit has a good selection of Cantonese and international sounds, including Chinese traditional, jazz, classical and contemporary music. It also offers a good range of VCDs of both Chinese films and Western movies with Chinese subtitles. ☎ 2845 7088, 2530 9696 ⌧ Shop 252, 2nd fl, Pacific Place, 88 Queensway, Admiralty ☺ 10am-8.30pm Mon-Thu, 10am-9pm Fri-Sun Ⓜ Admiralty 🚇 Yes

Yuet Wah Music Company (3, C4)
Yuet Wah Music Company is one of the few shops in Hong Kong selling quality Chinese music instruments at competitive prices – from the two-stringed *yi woo* (two-stringed musical instrument played upright with a bow) to *goo* (drums) and *bat* (brass cymbals). ☎ 2385 6880 ⌧ Ground fl, On Cheong Bldg, 464 Nathan Rd, Tsim Sha Tsui ☺ 9.30am-7pm Ⓜ Yau Ma Tei

Alt Malls
Crammed into buildings, up escalators and in back lanes are Hong Kong's malls of micro-shops selling designer threads, a kaleidoscope of kooky accessories and an Imelda Marcos of funky footwear. This is where Hong Kong's youngest mall-trawlers shop for clothes and trinkets or just to capture their moment of retail therapy on sticker machines. The best shopping is done from 3pm to 10pm, when *all* shops are open.

Beverley Commercial Centre (3, D7; 87-105 Chatham Rd, Tsim Sha Tsui)
Island Beverley (5, B4; 1 Great George St, Causeway Bay)
Rise Commercial Centre (3, D7; 5-11 Granville Circuit, Tsim Sha Tsui)
Trendy Zone (3, B2; Chow Tai Fook Centre, 580a Nathan Rd, Mong Kok)
Update Mall (3, C8; 36-44 Nathan Rd, Tsim Sha Tsui)

PHOTOGRAPHIC EQUIPMENT

When shopping for a camera or camcorder, never buy one that doesn't have a price tag. One of the best spots for buying photographic equipment is Stanley St (6, B2) in Central.

Color Six (6, C2)
Outlet with reliable photo processing (slides take just three hours) and professional film for sale. Prices aren't the lowest in town but the service is top quality. ☎ 2526 0123 🖥 www.colorsix.com ⌧ Ground fl, Shell Bldg, 18a Stanley St, Central ☺ 8.30am-7pm Mon-Fri, 8.30am-4pm Sat Ⓜ Central

Hing Lee Camera Company (6, B2)
A reputable outlet with new and second-hand 35mm camera bodies and lenses, as well as mid-range compact and digital cameras.

☎ 2544 7593 ✉ 25 Lyndhurst Tce, Central ☼ 9.30am-7pm Mon-Sat, 11am-5pm Sun Ⓜ Central

Onesto Photo Company (3, C7)
Also known as the Kimberley Camera Company, this retail outlet has price tags on the equipment (a rare

find in Tsim Sha Tsui) – but there's always latitude for bargaining.
☎ 2723 4668 ✉ Shop 2, Ground fl, Champagne Court, 16 Kimberley Rd, Tsim Sha Tsui ☼ 10am-9pm Ⓜ Tsim Sha Tsui

Photo Scientific (6, C2)
The favourite of Hong Kong's professionals. You

may find cheaper equipment elsewhere, but Photo Scientific has a rock-solid reputation, with labelled prices, no bargaining, no arguing and no cheating.
☎ 2525 0550 🖥 www .yp.com.hk/photoscientific ✉ Ground fl, Eurasia Bldg, 6 Stanley St, Central ☼ 9am-7pm Mon-Sat Ⓜ Central

Traditional Medicine

The Chinese have been using traditional medicine for over three millennia and it's very popular in Hong Kong, both for prevention and cure. Mixtures might include fungi, buds, seeds and roots or even deer antlers or snake blood. The main body is the **Chinese Medicine Council of Hong Kong** (☎ 2121 1888; www.cmchk.org .hk). **Eu Yan Sang** (6, B1; ☎ 2544 3870; 152-156 Queens Rd, Central) is probably the town's most famous practice. Be warned that endangered animals sometimes fall victim to traditional medicine men, although this is outlawed in Hong Kong.

SOUVENIRS & GIFTS

The markets (p35) are also hot spots for souvenir shoppers.

Alan Chan Creations (3, C9)
Alan Chan has designed everything from airport logos to soy sauce bottles, and he now lends his name to stylish accessories and ceramics. Some he has a hand in, others he simply approves of.
☎ 2723 2722 ✉ Shop 5A, Basement, Peninsula Hong Kong, Salisbury Rd, Tsim Sha Tsui ☼ 10am-7pm Ⓜ Tsim Sha Tsui

Chinese Arts & Crafts (3, B9)
This Aladdin's department store of souvenirs is probably the best place to buy quality bric-a-brac and other Chinese chotchkies (cheap, flashy trinkets). There are

four other branches including one at Pacific Place (4, E4), Admiralty.
☎ 2735 4061 🖥 www .crcretail.com ✉ 1st fl, Star House, 3 Salisbury Rd, Tsim Sha Tsui ☼ 10am-9.30pm 🚢 Star Ferry (Tsim Sha Tsui) Ⓜ Tsim Sha Tsui

Design Gallery (7, B1)
Supported by the Hong Kong Trade Development Council, this shop showcases local design in the form of jewellery, toys, ornaments and gadgets. It's a somewhat chaotic – but often rewarding – gaggle of goodies.
☎ 2584 4146 ✉ Hong Kong Convention and Exhibition Centre,

1 Harbour Rd, Wan Chai ☼ 10am-7pm Mon-Fri, 10am-6.30pm Sat 🚢 Star Ferry (Wan Chai) Ⓜ Wan Chai

King & Country (4, E4)
This shop has models and miniatures, mostly of a military bent (the American War of Independence and so forth). There are also street models of old Hong Kong: building frontages, a Chinese wedding procession, even an *'amah* (maid) with baby and chicken'.
☎ 2525 8603 🖥 www .kingandcountry.com ✉ Shop 362, 3rd fl, Pacific Place, 88 Queensway, Admiralty ☼ 10.30am-8pm Mon-Sat, 11am-7pm Sun Ⓜ Admiralty 🐾 Yes

Liuligongfang (4, C3)
Exquisite coloured objects, both practical (glasses, bowls, candle holders) and ornamental (figurines, crystal Buddhas, breathtaking sculptures) from a renowned Taiwan glass sculptress. There's a branch in Pacific Place, Admiralty (4, G9).
☎ 2973 0820 🖳 www .liuli.com ✉ Shop 20-22, Ground fl, Central Bldg, 1-3 Pedder St, Central ⌚ 10am-7.30pm Mon-Sat, 10am-7pm Sun Ⓜ Central 🚻 yes

Mandarin Oriental Flower & Gift Shop (4, D3)
This shop in the Mandarin Oriental has crockery, cushion covers, chopsticks, tasteful souvenirs and a small selection of jewellery, all of the highest quality.
☎ 2840 1974 ✉ Shop 13-14, 1st fl, Mandarin

Oriental, 5 Connaught Rd, Central ⌚ 8.30am-7.30pm Mon-Fri, 9am-6pm, Sat, 10am-5pm Sun ⛴ Star Ferry (Central) Ⓜ Central 🚻 Yes

Mountain Folkcraft (6, C2)
One of the nicest shops in town for folk crafts. This place has batik, clothing, woodcarvings and lacquerware made by Asian ethnic minorities. The shop attendants are friendly, and prices, while not cheap, are not outrageous either.
☎ 2523 2817 ✉ 12 Wo On Lane, Central ⌚ 9.30am-6.30pm Mon-Sat Ⓜ Central

Wah Tung Ceramic Arts (4, F4)
The world's largest supplier of hand-decorated ceramics, Wah Tung has some 18,000 items on display at

The perfect gift for a tea-aholic

this showroom just east of Pacific Place. You'll find everything from brightly painted vases and ginger jars to reproduction Tang dynasty figurines.
☎ 2520 5933 🖳 www .wahtungchina.com ✉ 8 Queen's Rd East, Admiralty ⌚ 10am-8pm Mon-Sat, 11am-7pm Sun Ⓜ Admiralty 🚻 Yes

SPORTING EQUIPMENT

Giga Sports (3, A9)
A large range of sports equipment, backpacks, clothing and footwear.
☎ 2115 9930 ✉ Shop 244-247, 2nd fl, Ocean Terminal, Harbour City, Canton Rd, Tsim Sha Tsui ⌚ 10am-8pm ⛴ Star Ferry (Tsim Sha Tsui) Ⓜ Tsim Sha Tsui

KS Ahluwalia & Sons (3, C8)
This store is well stocked with golf gear, tennis racquets, cricket bats, shirts and balls. It's cash only and no prices are marked, so haggle away.

☎ 2368 8334 ✉ 8c Hankow Rd, Tsim Sha Tsui ⌚ 10am-7.30pm Mon-Sat, 10am-5pm Sun Ⓜ Tsim Sha Tsui

Ming's Sports Company (3, C8)
This is an excellent place to buy gear for tennis or golf.
☎ 2376 1387 🖳 www .mingsports.com.hk ✉ 53 Hankow Rd, Tsim Sha Tsui ⌚ 9.30am-8pm Mon-Sat, 11am-6pm Sun Ⓜ Tsim Sha Tsui

Ocean Sky Divers (3, C8)
This shop, despite its somewhat ambiguous name, has

the whole range of diving and snorkelling gear.
☎ 2366 3738 🖳 www .oceanskydiver.com ✉ 1st fl, 17-19 Lock Rd, Tsim Sha Tsui ⌚ 10.30am-9pm Ⓜ Tsim Sha Tsui

Wise Mount Sports Co (3, C1)
A reputable family-run shop with camping gear, swimming goggles, pocket knives, compasses, hard-wearing bags and sports trophies.
☎ 2787 3011 ✉ 75 Sai Yee St, Mong Kok ⌚ 11.30am-10.30pm Ⓜ Mong Kok

Eating

There's a saying that the only thing with four legs that a Chinese won't eat is a table. Research suggests that the only winged object considered inedible is an aeroplane and anything underwater is fair game. This collective passion for eating makes Hong Kong one of the world's great cities for food. Grab your chopsticks and an empty bowl and tuck in.

Cuisines

The vast majority of Hong Kong's 10,000-odd restaurants are Chinese. Cantonese is by far the most popular Chinese cuisine in Hong Kong, but Chiu Chow, Shanghainese and Northern food is also easy to find. Cantonese cuisine is famously fresh: there's an emphasis on freshly slaughtered meat (mostly pork and chicken) and seafood. Simple techniques such as steaming and stir-frying allow the ingredients to retain their delicate and well-balanced flavours. Chiu Chow cuisine makes liberal use of garlic, vinegar and sauces; it's famous for goose and seafood dishes. Shanghainese cooking uses a lot of salted and preserved foods and relies on stewing, braising and frying. Northern Chinese food uses a lot of oils (eg sesame and chilli) coupled with ingredients such as vinegar, garlic, spring onions, bean paste and dark soy sauce. Steamed bread, dumplings and noodles are preferred to rice; and lamb and mutton, seldom seen on other Chinese menus, are also popular.

Hong Kong is loaded with budget and mid-range Chinese restaurants, and the top restaurants are usually in hotels. If you're having a bad noodle day, don't despair: Hong Kong is where East eats West and you'll find bangers 'n' mash and lasagne before you can say 'beef tendon congee'. Central is the best pick for Western restaurants, especially Soho, though you'll also find a fair few in Tsim Sha Tsui. In this chapter, restaurants with good or wholly vegetarian selections are marked with the **V** icon.

Meal Costs

For quick and inexpensive eats in Hong Kong follow the locals into the noodle restaurants with everything on the boil and steamed-up windows. More sophisticated Chinese, Asian and Western restaurants are usually pricier. Keep in mind that many restaurants have value-priced set lunches, but beware that straying from this will incur a cost – especially at top-end restaurants, where a bottle of water can easily add $40 to the bill. The price scale following represents the cost of an average dinner with a glass of wine or beer.

$	under $100
$$	$100-250
$$$	$250-400
$$$$	over $400

Noodles of every shape and size

Etiquette

Dining in Hong Kong is an all-in affair: everyone shares dishes, chats loudly and makes a mess. Food is to be enjoyed whole-heartedly, not picked at discreetly. There are, however, a few points of etiquette it doesn't hurt to know about.

- Wait for others to start before digging in (though as a guest you may well be asked to start).
- Say thank you if someone puts food into your bowl – this is a very kind and courteous gesture.
- Cover your mouth when using a toothpick.
- Don't reach for tasty morsels from the far side of dishes – what's closest to you is yours.
- Don't try to clean up dishes and detritus – a stained tablecloth is a sign of a good meal.
- Don't be afraid to ask for a fork if you can't manage chopsticks; nearly all Chinese restaurants have them.
- Don't stick chopsticks into a bowl as they resemble incense sticks in a bowl of ashes – a sign of death.
- Don't flip a fish over to reach the flesh on the bottom as the next fishing boat you pass will capsize.

Drinks

The most common liquid accompaniment to a Chinese meal is tea. It's drunk from the meal's beginning to end from a pot that is refilled from time to time. Beer is available almost everywhere, but wine doesn't start to feature until you're in mid-range to top-end places. Top Chinese restaurants pay great attention to their wine lists, but the mark-ups can be killers. Western restaurants tend to have smaller lists with a couple of reasonable tipples available by the glass.

Booking & Tipping

It's advisable to book ahead in all but the cheapest restaurants, especially on Friday and Saturday nights. Most restaurants add a 10% service charge. If the service was outstanding at an expensive restaurant (but never a cheap or mid-range place) you might consider adding another 5% or 10% on top of the service charge.

Kid-Friendly Kitchens

Children are generally welcome in Hong Kong's restaurants – especially Chinese ones – and we've indicated those that are particularly family friendly (or say they are!) with a 🖈 symbol in reviews. Few restaurants have highchairs or booster seats, however, so bring your own if you can't do without, or rely on a couple of telephone directories. Though most restaurants don't do special children's servings, Chinese food is generally shared and it's easy to create your own munchkin-sized portion.

The Dirt on Dim Sum

Yum cha (literally 'drink tea') is the usual way to refer to dim sum, the uniquely Cantonese 'meal' eaten as breakfast, lunch or brunch between about 7am and 2pm. Eating dim sum is a social occasion, consisting of many separate dishes that are meant to be shared. The bigger group you are with, the better.

Dim sum delicacies are normally steamed in small bamboo baskets. In most dim sum restaurants nowadays you order from a menu, but in older-style places the baskets are stacked up on pushcarts and rolled around the dining room. Just stop the waiter and choose something from the cart. Each pushcart has a different selection, so stagger your choices to give your stomach a fair go. It is said that there are up to 1000 dim sum dishes, but you'd be doing extremely well to sample 10 in one sitting.

The 10th floor of Times Square shopping centre in Causeway Bay (5, A4) has four Cantonese restaurants with dim sum, including the elegant **Heichinrou** (☎ 2506 2333; $$). If you want clatter and clutter, however, try **Maxim's Palace** (4, E3; ☎ 2521 1303; Hong Kong City Hall; $-$$).

Other dim sum destinations include **Yung Kee** (p69), **Lin Heung Tea House** (p71), **Chinese Restaurant** (p76), **Sweet Dynasty** (p78), **Wan Loong Court** (p79) and **Wu Kong Shanghai Restaurant** (p79).

Dim sum dishes include:

cha siu bau – barbecued pork buns
cheung fan – steamed rice-flour rolls with shrimp, beef or pork
ching chau sichoi – fried green vegetable of the day
chun guen – fried spring rolls
fan gwo – steamed dumplings with pork, shrimp and bamboo shoots
fu pei gun – crispy beancurd rolls
gaisi chaumin – fried crispy noodles with shredded chicken
gon siu yimin – dry-fried noodles
ha gau – shrimp dumplings
ho yip fan – rice wrapped in lotus leaf
pai gwat – steamed spare ribs
san juk ngau yok – steamed minced-beef balls
siu mai – pork and shrimp dumplings
woo gok – deep-fried taro balls

HONG KONG ISLAND

Central

Beirut (6, C2) $$$
Lebanese
Beirut is an affable, slightly cramped Lebanese restaurant that looks out onto Lan Kwai Fong. It serves authentic Lebanese dishes such as *kibbeh* (Lebanese meatballs) and *lahme bil agine* ('pizza' with minced lamb). The service is quite good for such a bustling place.
☎ 2804 6611
✉ Shop A, 27-39 D'Aguilar St ⏱ noon-3pm & 6-11.30pm Mon-Sat, 6-11pm Sun
Ⓜ Central

Bombay Dreams (6, B2) $$$
Indian
This place is not as all-singin', all dancin' as its Broadway namesake, but it's convenient to the pubs of Lan Kwai Fong and serves relatively authentic Indian fare in upmarket surrounds.

☎ 2971 0001 ✉ 1st fl, Carfield Commercial Bldg, 75-77 Wyndham St ◷ 12.30-2.30pm Mon-Sat, 6.30pm-10.30pm Mon-Sun Ⓜ Central Ⓥ

Café (4, D3) $$$
International
Formerly known as the Mandarin Coffee Shop, this place changed the face of what are called PPHR (popular-priced hotel restaurants) in the trade. The food is unswervingly excellent, and the service seamless.
☎ 2522 0111 ✉ Ground fl, Mandarin Oriental Hotel, 5 Connaught Rd Central ◷ 6.30am-12.45am Ⓜ Central ♿

China Lan Kwai Fong (6, C3) $$$
Chinese
China LKF's menu is as broad as its name suggests but it gratefully indicates the provenance of each dish. It's a pretty place, with caged songbirds, Chinese antique furnishings and excellent service.
☎ 2536 0968 ✉ 17-22 Lan Kwai Fong ◷ noon-3pm & 6pm-midnight Sun-Thu, 6pm-1am Fri & Sat Ⓜ Central

Cul-de-Sac (6, C2) $
American Fast Food
This is a well-run little place that offers fish and chips and pizza slices, but basically the repertoire sticks to burgers, sandwiches and submarines ($58 to $68).
☎ 2525 8116 ✉ 17 Wing Wah Lane ◷ 11am-1am Sun-Thu, 11am-3.30am Fri & Sat Ⓜ Central ♿

Eating Plus (4, D2) $$
International
Style comes cheap at this very vogue eatery and bar. Breakfasts are a snip ($27 to $32) – omelettes are fluffy, juices are freshly squeezed – and lunch and dinner, taken at communal tables, extend to soups, noodles (a successful mix of East and West) and rice dishes.
☎ 2868 0599 ✉ Shop 1009, 1st fl, IFC Mall, 1 Harbour View St ◷ 7.30am-10pm Ⓜ Central ♿ Ⓥ

Good Luck Thai (6, B2) $
Thai/Cantonese
After sinking a few beers in Lan Kwai Fong, make your way over to this chaotic but friendly place at the slops end of the charmingly nicknamed Rat Alley for a cheap fix of late-night Thai food. There is a fair number of Chinese dishes on offer too.
☎ 2877 2971 ✉ 13 Wing Wah Lane ◷ 11am-2am Mon-Sat, 4pm-midnight Sun Ⓜ Central ♿

Hunan Garden (4, D3) $$$
Hunanese
This elegant restaurant specialises in spicy Hunanese cuisine. The fried chicken with chilli is excellent, as are the seafood dishes. Views, overlooking the Victoria Harbour or into

Munch on meatballs and watch Lan Kwai Fong come alive

Perhaps not the friendliest faces, but who cares when the dim sum is this good

the heart of Central, are an added bonus.
☎ 2868 2880 ✉ 3rd fl, The Forum, Exchange Square, Connaught Rd Central ⏲ 11.30am-3.30pm & 5.30-11.30pm Ⓜ Central Ⓥ

Luk Yu Tea House (6, C2) $$
Dim Sum
This old-style teahouse is a museum piece in more ways than one. Most of the staff have been here since the early Ming dynasty and are as grumpy and ill-tempered as an emperor deposed. The booths are uncomfortable, it's not cheap, and prices aren't marked on the English menu – but the dim sum (7am to 6pm) is tasty.

☎ 2523 5464 ✉ 24-26 Stanley St ⏲ 7am-10pm Ⓜ Central ♿

M at the Fringe (6, C3) $$$$
International
No one seems to have a bad thing to say about Michelle's. The menu changes constantly, and everything is excellent, be it crab soufflé or slow-baked salted lamb. It's worth saving room for dessert, if you have that kind of self-restraint. Reservations are a must.
☎ 2877 4000 ✉ 1st fl, Fringe Club, Dairy Farm Bldg, 2 Lower Albert Rd ⏲ lunch noon-2.30pm Mon-Fri, dinner 7-10.30pm Mon-Sat, 7-10pm Sun Ⓜ Central Ⓥ

Mix (4, D4) $
International
A good and convenient spot to grab a meal on the fly or munch while surfing the in-house Internet. There's a branch in the IFC Mall (4, D2), Central.
☎ 2523 7396 ✉ Shop 11, The Cascade, Standard Chartered Bank Bldg, 3 Queen's Rd Central ⏲ 7am-9.30pm Mon-Thu, 7am-8pm Fri & Sat, 9.30am-7pm Sun Ⓜ Central ♿ Ⓥ

Rugheta (6, B2) $$$
Italian
This new kid on the block with a branch in New York City serves faultless Roman (read 'earthy Italian') cuisine.
☎ 2537 7922 ✉ Basement, Carfield Commercial

Fit to a Tea
When your teapot is empty or running low and you want a refill of hot water, signal the waiter by taking the lid off the pot and resting it on the handle. Legend tells us that this custom arose when a diner decided to keep his prize pigeon warm in his empty teapot without removing the lid. When the waiter refilled the pot he boiled the bird.

If you wish to thank the waiter, tap the table with three fingers. The middle finger represents a bowed head and the other fingers prostrate arms.

Bldg, 75-77 Wyndham St ☽ noon-3pm Mon-Sat, 7pm-midnight daily Ⓜ Central

Soho Soho (6, A3) $$$
British
More Boho (Below Hollywood Rd) than its namesake since its move a couple of hundred metres north, this place serves creative and comforting British food (crumpet with goat's cheese, herb-crusted roasted cod with new potatoes) to expats and Chuppies (Chinese yuppies). Excellent weekend brunch.
☎ 2147 2618 ✉ Ground fl, Work Station, 43-45 Lyndhurst Tce ☽ noon-2.30pm & 6.30-10.30pm Ⓜ Central

Va Bene (6, C3) $$$
Italian
This smart restaurant looks strikingly like a neighbourhood trattoria. A good choice for a special date or an extravagant celebration. Book ahead; dress smart.
☎ 2845 5577 ✉ 58-62 D'Aguilar St ☽ noon-3pm daily,

Late-Night Bites

Most restaurants stop serving meals at about 11pm but some won't let the chefs go home until the wee hours. Lan Kwai Fong (p66) is the best place for nocturnal dining, and snacking though the streets of Yau Ma Tei and Mong Kok (p79) also offers some choices. Take your insomniac stomach to these late-night spots: **Cul-de-Sac** (p67), **Good Luck Thai** (p67), **Global Forever Green Taiwanese Restaurant** (p74), **Good Hope Noodle** (p80) and **369 Shanghai Restaurant** (p72).

6.30-11.30pm Sun-Thu, 6.30pm-12.30am Fri & Sat Ⓜ Central

Vong (4, D3) $$$$
Fusion
A jewel of a restaurant in a jewel of a hotel, dramatically situated Vong features a creative mix of Vietnamese, Thai and French. Consider the tasting menu ($550) to get a full appreciation of the combination of French techniques with Asian flavours. Herbivores will appreciate the extensive vegetarian menu.
☎ 2825 4028 ✉ 25th fl, Mandarin Oriental Hotel, 5 Connaught Rd Central

☽ noon-3pm Mon-Fri, 6pm-midnight daily Ⓜ Central Ⓥ

Yung Kee (6, C2) $$
Cantonese
This long-standing institution is probably the most famous Cantonese restaurant in Central. Yung Kee's roast goose has been the talk of the town since 1942 (it farms its own birds for quality control), and its dim sum (2pm to 5pm) is excellent. The army of staff stay on their toes.
☎ 2522 0631 ✉ 32-40 Wellington St ☽ 11am-11.30pm Ⓜ Central ♿

Soho & Sheung Wan
2 Sardines (6, A2) $$$
French
This independent French bistro deserves the crowds it draws. The namesake fish comes grilled with a yoghurt sauce; the roasted rack of lamb is worth trying too. The wine list leans predictably to the Gallic side and is well chosen. Set lunches are excellent value.
☎ 2973 6618 ✉ 43 Elgin St, Soho ☽ noon-2.30pm & 6-10.30pm Ⓜ Central

Tempt your tastebuds at Michelle's

Meat-Free Dining

There are at least 100 dedicated vegetarian restaurants in Hong Kong, many of which boldly state their vegetarianism in gaudy neon so there's no confusion. **Miu Gute Cheong Vegetarian Restaurant** (p80) and **Joyful Vegetarian** (p80) are meat-free. **Kung Tak Lam** (p74) uses 100% organic produce in its vegetarian dishes. Other places with good awareness of vegetarian needs are **Gaylord** (p77), **M at the Fringe** (p68) and **Vong** (p69). Restaurants recommended for their vegetarian options in this chapter will be marked with a Ⓥ icon.

Blowfish (6, A2) $$
Japanese

This classy Japanese eatery, with its long sushi bar and enviable selection of sake, is a colourful, cool hang-out.
☎ 2815 7868 ✉ 20-26 Peel St, Soho 🕒 noon-2.30pm Mon-Sat, 6-10.30pm Mon-Thu, 6-11.30pm Fri & Sat Ⓜ Central

Boca (6, A2) $$$
Spanish

Sitting at the very end of Elgin St and boasting a wide frontage, Boca is a prime locale to watch the Soho parade. Weekend brunch is a favourite with or without champers ($245/109).
☎ 2548 1717 ✉ 65 Peel St, Soho 🕒 noon-3pm Mon-Fri, 11am-4pm Sat & Sun, 5pm-midnight daily Ⓜ Central Ⓥ

Grand Stage (4, A2) $$$
Cantonese

This hilarious place, with balcony and booth seating overlooking a huge dance floor in Western Market, features ballroom music and dancing at high tea and dinner. The food is acceptable but come here primarily to kick your heels up.
☎ 2815 2311 ✉ 2nd fl, Western Market, 323 Des Voeux Rd Central, Sheung Wan 🕒 lunch 11.30am-2.30pm, high tea 2.30-6.15pm, dinner 7pm-midnight Ⓜ Central

India Today (6, A2) $$
Indian

This upstairs eatery in the thick of the frenzy of Elgin St has reasonable curries, tandoori dishes, ice-cold beer and a pleasant atmosphere.
☎ 2801 5959 ✉ 1st fl, Million City Bldg, 26-30 Elgin St, Soho 🕒 11.30am- 3pm & 6-11.30pm Ⓜ Central Ⓥ

Korea Garden (4, B2) $$$
Korean

This comfortable restaurant serves a delicious array of appetisers (dried fish, pickles, kimchi), which come

I just need that one final fresh ingredient...

as side dishes to the BBQ sizzling at your table.
☎ 2542 2339 ✉ 1st fl, Blissful Bldg, 247 Des Voeux Rd Central, Sheung Wan ⏰ 11.30am-3pm Mon-Sat, 5.30-11pm daily Ⓜ Central ♿

Le Rendez-vous (6, A2) $
French
Tiny nautically themed crepe house that also does baguettes, *croques-monsieur* and salads. The crepes come filled with classic combos like mushroom and cheese, along with spicier inventions for the more adventurous.
☎ 2905 1808 ✉ 5 Staunton St, Soho ⏰ 10am-midnight Ⓜ Central ♿ Ⓥ

Leung Hing Restaurant (4, A2) $$
Chiu Chow
The staple ingredients of Chiu Chow cuisine – shellfish, goose and duck – are extensively employed and delectably prepared at this very local place.
☎ 2850 6666 ✉ 32 Bonham Strand West, Sheung Wan ⏰ 7.30am-11pm Ⓜ Sheung Wan ♿

Lin Heung Tea House (6, A1) $
Cantonese
Older-style Cantonese restaurant packed with old men reading the newspaper, extended families and large office groups. There's decent dim sum served from trolleys so it's good for a late bite or a meal alone. Although it's a very local place, there is an English menu available.

☎ 2544 4556 ✉ 160-164 Wellington St, Central ⏰ 6am-10pm Ⓜ Central ♿

Orange Tree (6, A3) $$$
Dutch
Modern Dutch food served in a breezy russet setting in the higher reaches of the Central Escalator. Don't get stuck on the sausages – there are lighter dishes like smoked eel. For dessert there are always *poffertjes* (thick mini pancakes) on the menu.
☎ 2838 9352 ✉ 17 Shelley St, Soho ⏰ 4pm-10.30pm Sun-Thu, 4pm-11pm Fri & Sat Ⓜ Central Ⓥ

Yi Jiang Nan (6, A2) $$
Shanghainese & Northern Chinese
This place has excellent (and quite enlightened) Shanghainese and Northern Chinese cuisine. Meals are served on black wooden tables under birdcages moonlighting as lanterns. The service is helpful and friendly.
☎ 2136 0886 ✉ 33-35 Staunton St, Soho ⏰ noon-3pm & 6-11pm Ⓜ Central Ⓥ

The Peak
Cafe Deco (4, A6) $$$
International
The philosophy seems to be that views, live jazz (Monday to Saturday nights) and buzzy ambience are enough to keep the punters happy. And if you stick to cocktails and simple fresh food (oyster bar, sushi) you won't go wrong. Don't miss the extraordinary Sunday brunch ($250).

Lin Heung: a new meaning to the word 'bustling'

☎ 2849 5111 ✉ Levels 1 & 2, Peak Galleria, 118 Peak Rd; ⏰ 11.30am-midnight Mon-Thu, 11.30am-1am Fri & Sat, 9.30am-midnight Sun 🚌 15 (from Exchange Sq), minibus 1 (from City Hall) 🚃 yes Ⓥ

Mövenpick Marché (4, A6) $$
International
Wander over and order from hawker 'stalls' offering everything from noodles and teppanyaki to pasta and sausages. It has several different eating areas, most of them with spectacular views of the harbour. This is a great place to bring kids: there's a play area and lots of child-friendly food.
☎ 2849 2000 ✉ Levels 6 & 7 (lift from Level 4), Peak Tower, 128 Peak Rd ⏰ 11am-11pm Mon-Fri, 9am-11pm Sat & Sun 🚌 15 (from Exchange Sq), minibus 1 (from City Hall) 🚃 yes ♿ Ⓥ

Eating When High

If (like us) you're a sucker for a view, you're going to love Hong Kong. The best ground-level views are looking across the harbour at Central from Tsim Sha Tsui, especially from **Yü** (3, C9; ☎ 2721 1211; $$$$), the top-notch seafood restaurant in the waterfront Hotel Inter-Continental Hong Kong.

On Hong Kong Island, the best views are from on high. **R66** (4, G5; ☎ 2862 6166; 62nd fl, Hopewell Centre, 183 Queen's Rd East, Wan Chai; $$$) obeys the unwritten code of revolving restaurants by playing cheesy music and serving average buffets (lunch/dinner $88/288). It's best to roll up for an afternoon tea ($40 to $108) and go for a twirl in the light of day. To access the lipstick tube–like Hopewell Centre's outfacing bubble lifts, change at the 17th floor (lifts 27 and 28 in the alcove opposite lift 6).

If you want a bit more class and still stay on the island, try **Petrus** (p73).

Other restaurants good for gawping include **Hunan Garden** (p67), the eateries on **Victoria Peak** (p71), **Open Kitchen** (p73), **Felix** (p77) and the **Salisbury Dining Room** (p78).

Peak Lookout (4, A6) $$$
International, Asian
East meets West at the Peak, with everything from Indian and French to Thai and Japanese on offer. Stick to the oysters (a dozen varieties), the BBQ, and the views – which are to the south of the island, not over the harbour.
☎ 2849 1000 ✉ 121 Peak Rd ⏱ 10.30am-midnight Mon-Thu, 10.30am-1am Fri, 8.30am-1am Sat, 8.30am- midnight Sun ➡ 15 (from Exchange Sq), minibus 1 (from City Hall) ♿ Yes ♿

Admiralty & Wan Chai

369 Shanghai Restaurant (7, B3) $$
Shanghainese
Low-key Shanghainese eatery that's nothing like five-star but does the dumpling job well. It's family-run and there are some good comfy booths in the front window. It's open late too, so you can come here after a draining

dance. Try their signature hot and sour soup ($40 to $60) – a meal in itself.
☎ 2527 2343 ✉ 30-32 O'Brien Rd, Wan Chai ⏱ 11am-4am Ⓜ Wan Chai ♿

Amaroni's Little Italy (4, G5) $$
Italian-American
The first rule of Italian-American cuisine is 'make it big' – and Amaroni's doesn't disappoint, with servings of pasta, seafood and steak so large that they make the floor staff strain. Kids get a free feed during the week.
☎ 2891 8555 ✉ Shop 3 & 4, Ground fl, Wu Chung House, 213 Queen's Rd East, Wan Chai ⏱ 11am-11.30pm Sun-Thu, 11am-midnight Fri & Sat Ⓜ Wan Chai ♿

American Restaurant (7, A3) $$
Northern Chinese
This place, which chose its name to attract American sailors on R&R during the Vietnam War, has been

serving decent Northern Chinese cuisine for over half a century. As you'd expect, the Peking duck ($275) and the beggar's chicken ($310) are very good.
☎ 2527 7277 ✉ Ground fl, Golden Star Bldg, 20 Lockhart Rd, Wan Chai ⏱ 11am-11.30pm Ⓜ Wan Chai

Beijing Shui Jiao Wong (7, B3) $
Northern Chinese
The 'Dumpling King' serves the best (and cheapest) Northern-style dumplings, *guo tie* (pan stickers) and soup noodles in Hong Kong.
☎ 2527 0289 ✉ 118 Jaffe Rd, Wan Chai ⏱ 7am-11pm Mon-Sat, noon-11pm Sun Ⓜ Wan Chai ♿ Ⓥ

Carrianna Chiu Chow Restaurant (4, J4) $$$
Chiu Chow
For Chiu Chow food, the Carrianna, entered from Tonnochy Rd, still rates right up there after all these years. Try the cold dishes

(sliced goose with vinegar, crab claws), pork with tofu or Chiu Chow chicken.

☎ 2511 1282 ✉ 1st fl, AXA Centre, 151 Gloucester Rd, Wan Chai 🕐 11am-11.30pm Ⓜ Wan Chai ♿

Che's Cantonese Restaurant (7, A3) $$$
Cantonese
This excellent Cantonese restaurant serves many home-style delicacies and offers a special seasonal menu with a dozen additional dishes. It's highly recommended.

☎ 2528 1123 ✉ 4th fl, The Broadway, 54-62 Lockhart Rd, Wan Chai 🕐 11am-3pm & 6-11.30pm Ⓜ Wan Chai

Dynasty (7, B2) $$$
Cantonese
Stylish Cantonese restaurant that does a much-lauded daily dim sum. This is a good choice for business lunches; the atmosphere is more hum

and hush than the normal dim sum clatter.

☎ 2802 8888 ✉ 3rd fl, Renaissance Harbour View Hotel, 1 Harbour Rd, Wan Chai 🕐 11.30am-2.30pm & 6.30-10.30pm Ⓜ Wan Chai

Open Kitchen (7, A2) $$
International
When your cafeteria serves up delicious Indian, Malay and Italian meals, and you have a harbour view to marvel at while you munch, you know you're on the right track. Open Kitchen is a good, arty option for meals, snacks or drinks at the bar.

☎ 2827 2923 ✉ 6th fl, Hong Kong Arts Centre, 2 Harbour Rd, Wan Chai 🕐 11am-9pm Ⓜ Wan Chai ♿ Ⓥ

Petrus (4, E4) $$$$
French
With its head (and prices) in the clouds, Petrus is one of the finest restaurants in Hong Kong. Expect

traditional (not nouvelle) French cuisine and stunning harbour views. Coat and tie required for guys.

☎ 2820 8590 ✉ 56th fl, Island Shangri-La Hong Kong, Pacific Place, Supreme Court Rd, Admiralty 🕐 noon-2.30pm Mon-Sat, 6.30-11pm daily Ⓜ Admiralty

Steam and Stew Inn (4, G5) $$
Cantonese
The Inn serves 'home-style' Cantonese food – steamed, stewed or boiled. Try the steamed mushroom stuffed with minced pork and crabmeat sauce. All dishes are free of ghastly MSG.

☎ 2529 3913 ✉ Ground fl, Hing Wong Court, 21-23 Tai Wong St East, Wan Chai 🕐 11.30am-3pm Mon-Sat, 5.30-11pm daily Ⓜ Wan Chai ♿

Tan Ta Wan (4, F5) $$
Thai
This smallish restaurant on the border between

Forget about menus, just point

Discover nirvana in a teacup at Moon Garden

Admiralty and Wan Chai serves some of the most authentic Thai food in town.
☎ 2865 1178 ✉ Shop 9, Rialto Bldg, 2 Landale St, Wan Chai ◷ 11am-11pm Mon-Fri, noon-10.30pm Sat & Sun Ⓜ Admiralty, Wan Chai ♿

Yè Shanghai (4, E4) $$
Shanghainese
Street-level Shanghainese cuisine with a few tweaks. The cold drunken pigeon is a wine-soaked winner and the steamed dumplings are perfectly plump, but sometimes this restaurant goes for clatter over substance. Live music from 9.30pm Thursday to Saturday.
☎ 2918 9833 ✉ Shop 332, Level 3, Pacific Place, 88 Queensway, Admiralty ✉ 11.30am-3pm & 6-11.30pm Ⓜ Admiralty ♿ Ⓥ

Causeway Bay
Chuen Cheung Kui Restaurant (5, B4) $$
Hakka (Chinese)
Enlist a Cantonese dining companion or dive in bravely: not much English is spoken here and the food is challenging. The pulled chicken, a Hakka classic, is the dish to insist upon.
☎ 2577 3833 ✉ 108-120 Percival St ◷ 11am-midnight Ⓜ Causeway Bay

Genroku Sushi (5, A4) $$
Japanese
Genroku is Hong Kong's most exotic fast-food chain. The sushi tears around on a conveyor belt and is reasonably fresh. The only drawback is the potentially long wait for seats, especially during the manic 1pm to 2pm lunch hour.
☎ 2803 5909 ✉ 3 Matheson St ◷ 11.30am-2am Ⓜ Causeway Bay ♿

Global Forever Green Taiwanese Restaurant (5, B4) $$
Taiwanese
Said to be a favourite of actor/director Jackie Chan, Forever Green is Hong Kong's best Taiwanese restaurant, a cuisine that borrows heavily from Fujian cooking. Try such specialities as oyster omelette, fried bean curd and *sanbeiji* (three-cup chicken). Noodle dishes are particularly good value.
☎ 2890 3448 ✉ 93-95 Leighton Rd (enter from Sun Wui Rd) ◷ 6pm-4am Ⓜ Causeway Bay

Gogo Café (5, C4) $$
Fusion
East meets West for spaghetti with *mentaiko* (fish roe) or rice with home-made bolognaise. The theme here is part Japanese teahouse, part cool café, and the light meals and home-made desserts make Gogo a good place to re-energise between lunch and dinner.
☎ 2881 5598 ✉ 11 Caroline Hill Rd ◷ noon-11pm Mon-Sat Ⓜ Causeway Bay ♿ Ⓥ

Kung Tak Lam (5, B4) $$
Vegetarian Chinese
This long-established place, which serves Shanghai-style meatless dishes, is more modern-feeling than most vegetarian eateries in Hong Kong. All veggies are 100% organic and dishes are free of MSG.
☎ 2881 9966 ✉ Ground fl, Lok Sing Centre, 31 Yee Wo St ◷ 11am-11pm Ⓜ Causeway Bay ♿ Ⓥ

Moon Garden Tea House (5, B4) $$
Chinese
The simple cuppa reaches nirvana-level heights at Moon Garden. Choose from many brews then lose an afternoon perusing tea books, admiring antiques (all for sale), snacking on meticulous morsels or having set lunch or dinner and taking refills from the heated pot beside your table.
☎ 2882 6878 ✉ 5 Hoi Ping Rd ◷ noon-midnight Ⓜ Causeway Bay

Queen's Cafe (5, B4) $$
Russian
This smallish Russian eatery has been here since 1952, accounting for its subdued yet assured atmosphere. The

borscht and meat set meals are good or try the *zakuska* ($68 to $180), a mixture of Russian appetisers.

☎ 2576 2658 ✉ Shop D, Ground fl, Eton Tower, 8 Hysan Ave ⏱ noon-11.30pm Ⓜ Causeway Bay

Red Pepper (5, B4) $$$
Sichuanese
If you want to set your palate aflame, try this friendly, long-established eatery's Sichuan-style sliced pork in chilli sauce, accompanied by *dan dan min* (noodles in a spicy peanut broth). Also recommended are the deep-fried beans and sizzling prawns.

☎ 2577 3811 ✉ 7 Lan Fong Rd ⏱ 11.30am-midnight Ⓜ Causeway Bay

WasabiSabi (5, A4) $$$
Japanese
Excellent Japanese cuisine, impeccable service and an OTT interior. From cable vines through to rondo lounges and into the sweeping sushi bar, this is eclectic magnificence; even the faux birch forest behind the bar has gumption.

Coffee Concerns
Coffee in Hong Kong tends to be overpriced and of dubious quality. Nevertheless there are plenty of cafés catering to your caffeine needs, including **First Cup Coffee** (3, C8; ☎ 2316 7793; 12 Hankow Rd, Tsim Sha Tsui), **TW Café** (6, B2; ☎ 2544 2237, Shop 2, Ground fl, Capitol Plaza, 2-10 Lyndhurst St, Central) and the **Café** (p67). Expensive generic-tasting coffee is available from **Pacific Coffee Company** and **Starbucks** in just about every shopping mall. For a cheaper cup try the **Délifrance** chain.

☎ 2506 0009 ✉ 13th fl, Times Square, 1 Matheson St ⏱ noon-3pm & 6pm-midnight Sun-Thu, 6-11.30pm Fri & Sat Ⓜ Causeway Bay

Island South

Boathouse (2, C3) $$$
International
All aboard for nautical overload. Salads, bruschetta and Med-inspired mains make up the bulk of the fleet. Aim for sea views.

☎ 2813 4467 ✉ 86-88 Stanley Main St, Stanley ⏱ 11am-midnight Sun-Thu, 11am-1am Fri & Sat 🚌 6, 6A, 6X, 260 (from Exchange Sq) Ⓥ

Jumbo Floating Restaurant (2, A3) $$$
Chinese
Floating restaurants have made Aberdeen world famous. Jumbo's interior looks like Beijing's Imperial Palace crossed with a Las Vegas casino. Diners should view it not so much as a restaurant but as an institution, since the overpriced food leaves something to be desired. There's free boat transport for diners from the pier on Aberdeen Promenade and next to the Aberdeen Marina Club. Dim sum is served from 7.30am to 4.30pm Sunday.

☎ 2553 9111 ✉ Shum Wan Pier Dr, Wong

All aboard for nautical overload

Chuk Hang, Aberdeen 🕙 10.30am-11.30pm Mon-Sat, 7.30am-11.30pm Sun 🚌 70, 73, 973 ♿

Lucy's (2, C3) $$$
International

Easy-going place that doesn't overwhelm with choice but with quality. The menu changes frequently as fresh produce and inspiration arrive, but the offerings tend toward honest fusion rather than fancy flimflammery. There's

a good selection of wines by the glass. ☎ 2813 9055 ✉ 64 Stanley Main St, Stanley 🕙 noon-3pm & 7-10pm Mon-Fri, noon-4pm & 6.30-10pm Sat & Sun 🚌 6, 6A, 6X, 260 (from Exchange Sq) Ⓥ

Verandah (2, B3) $$$$
Continental, Asian

In the new-colonial bit of the wavy Repulse Bay condos, Verandah is hushed and formal with heavy

white tablecloths and demurely clinking cutlery. The brunch is famous (book well ahead), and the afternoon tea is the south side's best. ☎ 2812 2722 ✉ 1st fl, Repulse Bay, 109 Repulse Bay Rd, Repulse Bay 🕙 lunch noon-3pm Tue-Sat, brunch 11am-2.30pm Sun, afternoon tea 3-5.30pm Tue-Sat, 3.30-5.30pm Sun, dinner 6.30-11pm Tue-Sun 🚌 6, 6A, 6X, 260 (from Exchange Sq)

KOWLOON

Tsim Sha Tsui & Tsim Sha Tsui East

Busan Korean Restaurant (3, B8) $$
Korean

This authentic Korean BBQ place stands out among the competition in touristy Tsim Sha Tsui. ☎ 2376 3385 ✉ Ground fl, Kowloon Centre, 29 Ashley Rd, Tsim Sha Tsui 🕙 11.30am-3pm & 6-11.30pm Ⓜ Tsim Sha Tsui ♿

Chinese Restaurant (3, C8) $$$$
Cantonese

This attractive place has acquired a good reputation for its original Cantonese food. The seafood is great and the high ceilings and traditional booth seating – based on Chinese teahouses of the 1920s – make for an unusual dining experience. ☎ 2311 1234 ext 2881 ✉ 2nd fl, Hyatt Regency, 67 Nathan Rd, Tsim Sha Tsui 🕙 11.30am-3pm

& 6.30pm-1am Mon-Sat, 10.30am-3pm Sun Ⓜ Tsim Sha Tsui ♿ Ⓥ

Dai Pai Dong (3, B7) $
Hong Kong

This modern version of a *cha chan tang*, a uniquely Hong Kong café with local dishes and snacks, serves meals throughout the day, but it's best to come at afternoon tea (2.30pm to 5.30pm) for such oddities as *yuan yang* (equal parts coffee and black tea with milk), boiled

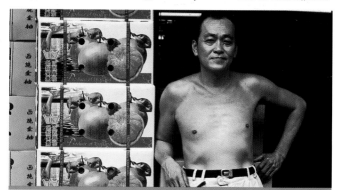

Kowloon City's streets are packed with postprandial delights like this...

Kowloon City

The neighbourhood of Kowloon City (2, B1), Hong Kong's Thai quarter, is worth a journey if you're looking for a tom yum or green curry fix. Among the simplest and most authentic (attracting Thai maids by the bucketful) is **Friendship Thai Food** (☎ 2382 8671; 38 Kai Tak Rd; $$). Nearby **Golden Orchard Thai Restaurant** (☎ 2716 1269; 12 Lung Kong Rd; $$) has spill-over rooms for when its restaurant fills up. The surrounding neighbourhood, packed with herbalists, jewellers, tea merchants and bird shops, is worth a postprandial look around.

cola with lemon and ginger, and toast smeared with condensed milk.
☎ 2317 7728 ✉ Ground fl, Hanley House, 70 Canton Rd, Tsim Sha Tsui ⏰ 7.30am-midnight Mon-Sat, 9am-midnight Sun Ⓜ Tsim Sha Tsui ♿

Dan Ryan's Chicago Grill (3, B9) $$$
American
The theme at Dan Ryan's is 'Chicago', including a model elevated rail system overhead and jazz and big-band music on the sound system. It is also one of the best places for burgers and ribs (half/full rack $132/198) in Hong Kong. There's also a branch in Pacific Place (4, E4) in Admiralty.
☎ 2735 6111 ✉ Shop 315, 3rd fl, Ocean Terminal, Harbour City, Canton Rd, Tsim Sha Tsui ⏰ 11am-midnight Mon-Fri, 10am-midnight Sat & Sun Ⓜ Tsim Sha Tsui ♿ Ⓥ

Dong (3, C7) $$$
Cantonese
It's the classic hotel restaurant interior right down to the chintzy music, but the menu at 'East' does offer adventurous Cantonese dishes, including

seafood soups and a forest of fungus.
☎ 2315 5166 ✉ Arcade Level 2, Miramar Hotel, 118-130 Nathan Rd, Tsim Sha Tsui ⏰ 11.30am-2.30pm Mon-Sat, 10.30am-3.30pm Sun, 6-10.30pm daily Ⓜ Tsim Sha Tsui Ⓥ

Fat Angelo's (3, B8) $$
Italian-American
Huge portions, free salads, unlimited bread and relatively low prices are the keys to success at this chain of Italian-American restaurants. There's also a branch on Elgin St (6, A2) in Soho.
☎ 2730 4788 ✉ 35 Ashley Rd, Tsim Sha Tsui ⏰ noon-midnight Ⓜ Tsim Sha Tsui ♿

Felix (3, C9) $$$$
Fusion
Felix has a fantastic setting, both inside and out. You're sure to pay as much attention to the views and the Philippe Starck–designed interior as the fusion food (think lobster nachos, hoisin grilled ribs). Towering ceilings and copper-clad columns surround the Art Deco tables. Even the view from the men's is dizzying.
☎ 2315 3188 ✉ 28th fl, Peninsula Hong Kong,

Salisbury Rd, Tsim Sha Tsui ⏰ 6pm-12.30am Ⓜ Tsim Sha Tsui Ⓥ

Gaylord (3, B8) $$$
Indian
Dim lighting and live Indian music set the scene for enjoying the excellent *rogan josh*, *dhal* and other favourite dishes at Hong Kong's oldest India restaurant. There are lots of vegetarian choices.
☎ 2376 1001 ✉ 1st fl, Ashley Centre, 23-25 Ashley Rd, Tsim Sha Tsui ⏰ noon-3pm & 6-11pm Ⓜ Tsim Sha Tsui ♿ Ⓥ

Genki Sushi (3, D7) $
Japanese
A branch of the popular (and inexpensive) sushi chain with a Japanese 'meany face' as its logo.
☎ 2722 6689 ✉ Shop G7-G9, Ground fl, East Ocean Centre, 98 Granville Rd, Tsim Sha Tsui East ⏰ 11.30am-11.30pm 🚌 5C, 8 (from Star Ferry pier) Ⓜ Tsim Sha Tsui ♿

Happy Garden Noodle & Congee Kitchen (3, B7) $
Cantonese
A choice of some 200 rice, noodle and congee dishes are offered, including shrimp wonton noodles ($28).

There's also main dishes such as beef in oyster sauce ($55) and roast duck ($45).
☎ 2377 2604 ✉ 76 Canton Rd, Tsim Sha Tsui ☯ 7am-2am Ⓜ Tsim Sha Tsui ♿ Ⓥ

Kyozasa (3, B8) $$
Japanese
This colourful and cosy Japanese restaurant has a menu that extends from sushi to steaks via hotpots. There are also reasonably priced set lunches.
☎ 2376 1888 ✉ 20 Ashley Rd, Tsim Sha Tsui ☯ noon-2.30pm & 6pm-midnight Ⓜ Tsim Sha Tsui Ⓥ

Orphée (3, D6) $$$
French
This minimalist but cosy restaurant is a small pocket of Paris in deepest Tsim Sha Tsui. If you feel like a fix of foie gras, this is your choice.
☎ 2730 1128 ✉ 18a Austin Ave, Tsim Sha Tsui ☯ noon-2.30pm & 6.45-10.15pm Ⓜ Jordan

Sabatini (3, E7) $$$$
Italian
Classy Sabatini is a direct copy of its namesake in Rome, with murals on the walls and ceilings and polished terracotta tiles on the floor. Even classic Italian dishes, such as fettuccine carbonara, come across as light in the best sense, leaving room to sample the exquisite desserts. The wine list is excellent but expensive.
☎ 2721 5215 ✉ 3rd fl, Royal Garden, 69 Mody Rd, Tsim Sha Tsui East ☯ noon-2.30pm & 6-11pm 🚌 5C, 8 (from Star Ferry pier) Ⓜ Tsim Sha Tsui ⚓ Tsim Sha Tsui East Ferry Pier

Salisbury Dining Room (3, C9) $$
International
Unlimited sushi and smoked salmon make the Salisbury lunch and dinner ($98 and $218) buffets a pretty good bet. Book ahead if you want a table by the window and unimpeded harbour views. Guzzlers should note that the buffets include bottomless glasses of draught beer.
☎ 2268 7000 ✉ 4th fl, Salisbury, 41 Salisbury Rd, Tsim Sha Tsui ☯ noon-2.30pm & 6.15-9.30pm Ⓜ Tsim Sha Tsui ♿ Ⓥ

Spring Deer (3, D8) $$
Northern Chinese
This is probably Hong Kong's most famous (if not salubrious) Peking restaurant and serves some of the crispiest Peking duck ($280 per bird) in town. Be sure to book well in advance.
☎ 2366 4012 ✉ 1st fl, 42 Mody Rd, Tsim Sha Tsui ☯ noon-3pm & 6-11pm Ⓜ Tsim Sha Tsui ♿

Spring Moon (3, C9) $$$$
Cantonese
The Peninsula's flagship Chinese restaurant, Spring Moon's décor is Japanese minimalist with bits of Art Deco thrown in. The Cantonese food is excellent, and the ambience is great.
☎ 2315 3160 ✉ 1st fl, Peninsula Hong Kong, Salisbury Rd, Tsim Sha Tsui ☯ lunch 11.30am-2.30pm Mon-Sat, 11am-3pm Sun, tea 3-4.30pm Mon-Sat, 3-5pm Sun, dinner 6-10.30pm daily Ⓜ Tsim Sha Tsui

Sweet Dynasty (3, B7) $
Cantonese
Sweet Dynasty has it all, from fine dim sum (weekends only) to tofu soups to bowls of congee big enough to swim in. It's a riot at lunch time but somehow, amidst all the clatter and kids, Sweet Dynasty retains a sense of style.
☎ 2199 7799 ✉ 88 Canton Rd, Tsim Sha Tsui ☯ 10am-midnight Mon-Thu, 10am-1pm Fri, 7.30am-1am Sat, 7.30am-midnight Sun Ⓜ Tsim Sha Tsui ♿ Ⓥ

A Touch of Spice (3, C7) $$
South-East Asian
This is one of several trendy restaurant/bars stacked up Japanese-style at 10 Knutsford Terrace. This one does Thai curries, Indonesian and Vietnamese noodles and stir-fried dishes. Most meals are good value, unless you go for the seafood.

Good things come from small kitchens

Saint's Alp Teahouse in Mong Kok

sum (11am to 3pm Monday to Friday, 11am to 6pm Saturday and Sunday) takes some beating. Stand-outs include the steamed beef with tangerine peel and grouper with lemongrass and minced squid. The house special dessert is t'ai chi cake (a chestnut paste and poppy seed pastry).
☎ 2734 3722 ✉ Lower Level 2, Kowloon Hotel, 19-21 Nathan Rd, Tsim Sha Tsui ⏲ 11am-3pm & 6-11pm Mon-Fri, 11am-11pm Sat & Sun Ⓜ Tsim Sha Tsui ♿ Ⓥ

Wu Kong Shanghai Restaurant (3, H6) $$
Shanghainese
The specialities at this Shanghainese restaurant – cold pigeon in wine sauce and crispy fried eels – are worth a trip across town. Dim sum is served all day.
☎ 2366 7244 ✉ Basement, Alpha House, 27-33 Nathan Rd, Tsim Sha Tsui ⏲ 11.30am-midnight Ⓜ Tsim Sha Tsui ♿

Yau Ma Tei & Mong Kok

Golden Bull (3, C1) $$
Vietnamese
This place is almost always packed. The punters are not

☎ 2312 1118 ✉ 1st fl, 10 Knutsford Tce, Tsim Sha Tsui ⏲ noon-11.30pm Mon-Sat, 6-11.30pm Sun Ⓜ Tsim Sha Tsui Ⓥ

Valentino (3, D8) $$$
Italian
This long-established *ristorante* is a romantic Italian classic with soft lights and nuzzling music. The seasonal menu has super

soups and a good range of salads, pasta and meats.
☎ 2721 6449 ✉ Ground fl, Ocean View Court, 27a Chatham Rd Sth, Tsim Sha Tsui ⏲ noon-11pm Ⓜ Tsim Sha Tsui Ⓥ

Wan Loong Court (3, C8) $$$
Cantonese
Wan Loong has wonderful Cantonese food with modern touches; the dim

Business with a Bite
A lot of expense-account wining and dining occurs at hotel restaurants: in Tsim Sha Tsui consider the Hyatt Regency's **Chinese Restaurant** (p76) or **Dong** (p77) at the Miramar Hotel. On Hong Kong Island, the Renaissance Harbour View's **Dynasty** (p73) is right by the Convention and Exhibition Centre, while **Vong** (p69) in the Mandarin Oriental is as central as it gets.

Good lunch spots where you can talk without shouting include **Rugheta** (p68) and the **Café** (p67). **M at the Fringe** (p68) and **Soho Soho** (p69) are great places to celebrate when you've sealed the deal.

Familiar Signs

You'll see signs for **Cafe de Coral, Maxim's, Dai Pai Dong, Fairwood** and **Saint's Alp** just about everywhere. These are local fast-food joints where you can get decent Chinese and Western meals in a flash for little cash. Among the best places for sandwiches, soups, salads and baked goods are branches of the **Oliver's Super Sandwiches** and **Délifrance** chains. **7-Eleven** outlets, on virtually every corner of the territory and open 24 hours, are good places for drinks and snacks on the go.

coming for the atmosphere (noisy) or service (abrupt), but the excellent-quality, reasonably priced Vietnamese dishes. There's a branch in Times Square (5, A4) in Causeway Bay.
☎ 2628 9288 ✉ Level 7, **Grand Century Place, 193 Prince Edward Rd West, Mong Kok** noon-11.30pm Ⓜ Prince Edward Ⓡ Mong Kok KCR East Rail Ⓥ

Good Hope Noodle (3, B1) $
Noodles
This busy noodle-stop is known far and wide for its terrific wonton soups and shredded pork noodles with spicy bean sauce. Good Hope Noodle is an eat-and-go sort of place – don't come here if you feel like lingering.
☎ 2394 5967 ✉ 146 **Sai Yeung Choi St Sth, Mong Kok** 11am-3am Ⓜ Mong Kok

Joyful Vegetarian Restaurant (3, B3) $
Chinese Vegetarian
Popular restaurant serving great all-vegetarian meals. The country-style hotpot is made with a wide range of fungi, and there's a snack counter facing the street.
☎ 2780 2230 ✉ 530 **Nathan Rd, Yau Ma Tei** 11am-11pm Ⓜ Yau Ma Tei Ⓥ

Kubrick Bookshop Cafe (3, B4) $
International Café
This café and bookshop next to the Broadway Cinematheque (p88) has a great range of film-related books, magazines and paraphernalia, and serves good coffee and decent pre-flick food such as sandwiches ($28 to $30) and pasta ($30 to $40).
☎ 2384 5465 ✉ **Broadway Cinematheque, 3 Public Sq St, Yau Ma Tei** 11.30am-10.30pm Ⓜ Yau Ma Tei Ⓥ

Miu Gute Cheong Vegetarian Restaurant (3, C5) $
Chinese Vegetarian
Cheap, cheerful and family-oriented vegetarian restaurant. The tofu is fresh and firm, the vegetables are the pick of the market and the tea flows freely.
☎ 2771 6218 ✉ 31 **Ning Po St, Yau Ma Tei** 11am-11pm Ⓜ Yau Ma Tei Ⓥ

Saint's Alp Teahouse (3, C1) $
Chinese Snacks
One in a chain of clean and very cheap snackeries in Hong Kong (look for the footprint logo). It's a great pit stop for Taiwanese-style frothy tea with tapioca drops and Chinese snacks such as shrimp balls, noodles and rice puddings.
☎ 2782 1438 ✉ 61a **Shantung St, Mong Kok** 11.30am-1am Ⓜ Mong Kok Ⓥ

Entertainment

When you want to be wowed after dark, Hong Kong is a capable entertainer. Most weeks, half a dozen local arts companies perform anything from Cantonese opera to an English-language version of a Chekhov play. The Hong Kong government subsidises the cost of most international acts, so ticket prices are generally very reasonable. Expect to pay around $50 for a seat up the back for the Hong Kong Philharmonic and from about $350 for an international musical like *Mamma Mia!*.

To find out what's on in Hong Kong, pick up a copy of *HK Magazine* (asiacity@asia-city.com.hk), a very comprehensive entertainment listings magazine. It's free, appears on Friday and can be found at restaurants, bars, shops and hotels. Also worth checking out is the freebie *bc magazine* (www.bcmagazine.net), a biweekly guide to Hong Kong's entertainment and partying scene. The **Hong Kong Arts Centre** (www.hkac.org.hk) publishes *Artslink*, a monthly with listings of performances, exhibitions and art-house film screenings.

Bookings for most cultural events can be made by telephoning **Urbtix** (☎ 2734 9009; www.urbtix.gov.hk; ☼ 10am-8pm). You can also book tickets for many films and concerts and a great variety of cultural events through **Cityline** (☎ 2317 6666; www.cityline.com.hk).

Tipped Top Spots

The best and most complete bar strip in Hong Kong is **Lan Kwai Fong** (6, C3), a narrow L-shaped alleyway in Central lined with bars and clubs. The clientele is relatively young and upwardly mobile, and expats mix easily with local business types and trendies. Nearby **Soho** (6, A2) has more of a restaurant scene and a number of bars have opened along the escalator route and its cross streets.

Wan Chai (7) is part sleaze territory, with awful hostess bars along Lockhart Rd, and part upbeat fun, with lots of zippy club action and late-night cover-band venues. It's the part of town that kicks on latest – handy if dawn is approaching and you still want to carry on.

Kowloon (3) has more of a local Chinese scene. There are three basic clusters of bars in **Tsim Sha Tsui**: along Ashley Rd (3, B8); Prat Ave and Hart Ave, just west of Chatham Rd Sth (3, D7); and Knutsford Terrace (3, C7). **Tsim Sha Tsui East** (3, E7) is swanky hostess-bar territory.

Check out the restaurant scene in lively Soho

Special Events
January/February *Chinese New Year* – late January/early February fireworks, flower fairs and international parade

Fringe Festival – eclectic performances sponsored by the Fringe Club (p90) over three weeks

Hong Kong Arts Festival – February month-long series of performing arts and exhibitions

International Marathon – held in Sha Tin (1, D1)

Spring Lantern Festival – colourful lantern festival marking the end of the Lunar New Year and the day for lovers

March *Hong Kong Rugby Sevens* – three-day carnival in late March; the territory's biggest sporting event

April *Hong Kong International Film Festival* – a cinematic showcase held over 16 days

Ching Ming – traditional festival in which families clean the graves of ancestors

April/May *Birthday of Tin Hau* – late April/early May celebrations on the water in honour of the patroness of fisherfolk

Cheung Chau Bun Festival – Taoist march, lunge and munch (see boxed text p37)

June *Dragon Boat Festival* – boat races and fireworks

July *Hong Kong Fashion Week* – mid-July parades and events at the Convention and Exhibition Centre (7, B1) and at shopping centres

August *International Arts Carnival* – focuses on the Cultural Centre (p91) with performances by and for children

Food Expo – festival of the munch at the Convention and Exhibition Centre (p31)

September *Mid-Autumn Festival* – mid-September romantic moon-watching celebration

October *Hong Kong Youth Arts Festival* – young talent perform at various venues

Chung Yeung Festival – picnics on hills and (more) family visits to graves

International Cricket Series – two-day event in late October/early November (p93)

November *Hong Kong Golf Open* – held at the Royal Hong Kong Golf Club (1, C1) at Fanling Golf Course in the New Territories

December *Christmas Day/Boxing Day* – tree decorating, turkey basting and gobbling

BARS & PUBS

Drinking venues in Hong Kong run the gamut from fairly authentic British-style pubs with meat pies, darts and warm beer to stylish lounges where the clothes are straight out of the bag, the sounds are smooth, the drinks are electric and the buzz is hardcore gossip. Much of Hong Kong's nightlife takes place in top-end hotels where inventive cocktails, skilled bar staff and some of the best views in town attract visitors and locals.

Bar (3, C9)
For mellow '40s and '50s jazz, take your smoking jacket along and sip cognac at the Peninsula's stylish Bar. Your fellow tipplers will be serious business types, coutured couples and new money trying to look old. Music starts around 9.30pm. ☎ 2315 3163 ✉ 1st fl, Peninsula Hong Kong, Salisbury Rd, Tsim Sha Tsui ⏰ 4pm-midnight Mon-Thu, 2pm-midnight Fri & Sat, 3pm-midnight Sun Ⓜ Tsim Sha Tsui

Biergarten (3, C8)
This clean modern place has a hits-and-misses jukebox and Bitburger on tap. It's popular with visiting Germans and others who hanker after Black Forest ham, pork knuckle and sauerkraut, and Wiener schnitzel. On fine days the front is opened to the street. ☎ 2721 2302 ✉ 5 Hanoi Rd, Tsim Sha Tsui ⏱ noon-2am (happy hr 4-9pm) Ⓜ Tsim Sha Tsui

Bit Point (6, B3)
Owned by the same lot as Biergarten, Bit Point is essentially a German-style bar, where beer drinking is taken very seriously. Most beers here are draught pilsners, which you can get in a glass boot if you've got a huge thirst to kick. ☎ 2523 7436 ✉ 31 D'Aguilar St ⏱ noon-3am Mon-Fri, noon-4am Sat, 4pm-2am Sun (happy hr 4-9pm) Ⓜ Central

Brecht's (5, B4)
This is a very small and fairly unusual club-like bar. It's an arty kind of place given more to intimate, cerebral conversation than serious raging. The décor is pseudo-German and includes oversized portraits of such charmers as Mao and Hitler. ☎ 2576 4785 ✉ Ground fl, Rita House, 123 Leighton Rd, Causeway Bay ⏱ 4pm-2am Sun-Thu, 4pm-4am Fri & Sat (happy hr 4-8pm) Ⓜ Causeway Bay

Bridge (7, A3)
This large and airy bar, with great windows overlooking the frenzy of Lockhart Rd, serves round-the-clocktails to the denizens and the doomed of Wan Chai. ☎ 2865 5586 ✉ 1st fl, Beverly House, 93-107 Lockhart Rd, Wan Chai ⏱ 24hr (happy hr noon-10pm) Ⓜ Wan Chai

Captain's Bar (4, D3)
This clubby, suited place in the Mandarin Oriental serves ice-cold draught beer in chilled silver mugs and some of the best martinis in town. It's a good place to talk business, at least until the band (covers Monday to Saturday, jazz on Sunday) strikes up at 9pm. ☎ 2522 0111 ✉ Ground fl, Mandarin Oriental, 5 Connaught Rd Central ⏱ 11am-2am Mon-Sat, 11am-1am Sun Ⓜ Central 🍴 yes

Champagne Bar (7, B2)
Take your fizz in the sumptuous surrounds of the Grand Hyatt's Champagne Bar, kitted out in Art Deco furnishings to evoke the Paris of the 1920s. Live blues or jazz rings through the bar most evenings and the circular main bar is always busy. ☎ 2588 1234 ext 7321 ✉ Ground fl, Grand Hyatt Hong Kong, 1 Harbour Rd, Wan Chai ⏱ 5pm-2am Ⓜ Wan Chai

Chapter 3 (6, B2)
This cheerful, very red bar defies its dungeon setting. It's stylish but far less trendy than most bars around here, maintaining a low-key feel and a loyal crowd.

Oars away!

☎ 2526 5566 ✉ Basement, Amber Lodge, 23 Hollywood Rd, Central (enter from Cochrane St) ⏱ 5pm-2am Sun-Thu, 5pm--5am Fri, 7pm-5am Sat (happy hr 5-10pm) Ⓜ Central

Chemical Suzy (3, D6)
This is a cyber-groover hide-out with DJs, snacks and enough pop-culture signifiers to leave no doubt that Suzy's in the know. Attracts a mixed crowd. ☎ 2736 0087 ✉ Ground fl, AWT Centre, 2a-2b Austin Ave, Tsim Sha Tsui ⏱ 6pm-4am (happy hr 6-9pm) Ⓜ Tsim Sha Tsui

China Bear (1, B2)
The China Bear is the most popular expatriate-run pub-restaurant on Lantau Island, and has a wonderful open bar facing the water from where you can watch yet another ferry that you should have boarded depart. It's got Boddington, Strongbow and lots of lagers on tap. ☎ 2984 9720 ✉ Ground fl, Mui Wo Centre, Ngan

Wan Rd, Mui Wo, Lantau Island ⏰ 10am-3am (happy hr 5-9pm Mon-Fri, 5-8pm Sat) 🚇 Mui Wo

Club 1911 (6, A2)

This is a very refined bar with fine details (stained glass, burlwood bar, ceiling fans) and some colonial nostalgia. ☎ 2810 6681 ✉ 27 Staunton St, Soho ⏰ 5pm-midnight Mon-Sat (happy hr 5-9pm) 🚇 Central

Club 64 (6, B2)

The name of this funky hang-out recalls the Tiananmen Square massacre of 4 June 1989; it's one of the best bars for those who want a simple, unfussy night out. ☎ 2523 2801 ✉ 12-14 Wing Wah Lane ⏰ 3pm-2am Mon-Thu, 3pm-3am Fri & Sat, 3pm-1am Sun (happy hr 3-9pm) 🚇 Central

Delaney's (7, A3)

At this immensely popular Irish watering hole you can choose between the ground floor pub tiled in black and white, or the sports bar

and restaurant on the 1st floor. The food is good and plentiful; the kitchen allegedly goes through 400kg of potatoes a week. There's also a branch on Peking Rd (3, C8) in Tsim Sha Tsui. ☎ 2804 2880 ✉ Ground & 1st fl, One Capital Place, 18 Luard Rd, Wan Chai ⏰ noon-2.30am Sun-Thu, noon-3.30am Fri-Sun (happy hr 5-9pm) 🚇 Wan Chai

Devil's Advocate (7, A3)

This pleasant pub in the thick of things in Wan Chai is as relaxed as they come. The bar spills on to the pavement and the staff are charming. ☎ 2865 7271 ✉ 48-50 Lockhart Rd, Wan Chai ⏰ noon-late Mon-Sat, 1pm-late Sun (happy hr noon-10pm) 🚇 Wan Chai

Dickens Bar (5, B3)

This evergreen place has been a popular place with expats and Hong Kong Chinese for decades. There's a curry buffet lunch ($98, including half a pint of beer) and lots of big-screen sports. ☎ 2837 6782 ✉ Base-

ment, Excelsior Hong Kong, 281 Gloucester Rd, Causeway Bay ⏰ 11am-1am Sun-Thu, 11am-2am Fri & Sat (happy hr 5-8pm) 🚇 Causeway Bay

Dragon-I (6, B3)

This fabulous venue on the edge of Soho has both an indoor bar and restaurant and a huge terrace over Wyndham St filled with caged songbirds. You'd almost think you were in the country. ☎ 3110 1222 ✉ Upper ground fl, Centrium, 60 Wyndham Street, Central ⏰ noon-midnight Mon-Sat (happy hr on terrace 6-9pm) 🚇 Central

Dublin Jack (6, B2)

This Irish pub is a very popular after-hours pub for expats. We like the mock-old 'Oirish village' frontage and the seamless service. ☎ 2543 0081 ✉ Ground fl, Cheung Hing Commercial Bldg, 37-43 Cochrane St ⏰ 11am-2am (happy hr 11am-9pm) 🚇 Central

Feather Boa (6, A2)

Feather Boa is a plush lounge hidden behind gold drapes. Part camp lounge, part bordello — part those curtains and order a mango daiquiri ($75). ☎ 2857 2586 ✉ 38 Staunton St, Soho ⏰ 5pm-late Tue-Sat ⏰ Central

Felix (3, C9)

Take a brew with an amazing view at the bar connected to Felix (p77), the Peninsula's swankiest restaurant. Guys, the design

Elbow in with the local barflies for a buzzy post-work cocktail

of the men's room is just beyond belief.
☎ 2315 3188 ✉ 28th fl, Peninsula Hong Kong, Salisbury Rd, Tsim Sha Tsui ☙ 6pm-2am Ⓜ Tsim Sha Tsui

Gecko (6, B2)
Relaxed hide-out run by a friendly French sommelier and wine importer with a penchant for absinthe. The well-hidden DJ mixes good grooves with kooky Parisian tunes, and there's live music on Tuesday and Wednesday.
☎ 2537 4680 ✉ Lower ground fl, 15-19 Hollywood Rd (enter from Ezra's Lane off Cochrane St or Pottinger St), Central ☙ 4pm-2am Mon-Thu, 4pm-4am Fri & Sat (happy hr 4-10pm) Ⓜ Central

Groovy Mule (7, A3)
This pulsating Aussie bar – staff in cork hats, no less – attracts punters with its never-ending happy hour.
☎ 2527 2077 ✉ 37-39 Lockhart Rd, Wan Chai ☙ 4pm-3am to 5am

Hari's (3, C8)
Is it tacky or classy (or neither)? You decide after you've had a couple of speciality martinis (there are over a dozen to challenge you). There's live music nightly, from 7.30pm to 12.30am Sunday to Thursday and to 1.15am at the weekend.
☎ 2369 3111 ext 1345 ✉ Mezzanine, Holiday Inn Golden Mile, 50 Nathan Rd, Tsim Sha Tsui ☙ 5pm-2am (happy hr 5-9pm Mon-Sat, 5pm-2am Sun) Ⓜ Tsim Sha Tsui

Inn Side Out & East End Brewery (5, B4)
These two pubs flank a central covered terrace where you can while away the hours on a warm evening, throwing peanut shells on the ground. East End has imported microbrews.
☎ 2895 2900 ✉ Ground fl, Sunning Plaza, 10 Hysan Ave, Causeway Bay ☙ 9am-1am Sun-Thu, 9am-1.30am Fri & Sat (happy hr 2.30-8.30pm) Ⓜ Causeway Bay

La Dolce Vita (6, C3)
This is a buzzy place for post-work cocktails with room to prop on the heart-shaped bar or stand on the terrace and watch the mob crawl by. 'The Sweet Life' offers about the best vantage point on the Fong.
☎ 2186 1888 ✉ Ground fl, Cosmos Bldg, 9-11 Lan Kwai Fong, Central ☙ 11am-2am Mon-Thu, 11.30am-3am Fri, 2pm-3am Sat, 2pm-1am Sun (happy hr 5.30-8pm) Ⓜ Central

Le Jardin (6, B2)
Don't imagine a breezy oasis – 'The Garden' is no more than an enclosed veranda – but this is still an attractive bar with loads of atmosphere. The predominantly expat crowd enjoys itself without getting too boisterous.
☎ 2526 2717 ✉ 1st fl, Winner Bldg, 10 Wing Wah Lane, Central ☙ noon-3am Mon-Thu, noon-4am Fri, 4.30pm-3am Sat (happy hr noon-8pm Mon-Fri, 4.30-8pm Sat) Ⓜ Central

Mes Amis (7, A3)
This easygoing bar is in the lap of girly club land. It has a good range of wines and a Mediterranean-style snack list. There's a DJ from 11pm on weekend nights.
☎ 2527 6680 ✉ 83 Lockhart Rd, Wan Chai ☙ noon-2am Sun-Thu, noon-5am Fri & Sat (happy hr 4-9pm) Ⓜ Wan Chai

Peak Cafe Bar (6, A2)
The fixtures and fittings of the much-missed Peak Cafe, from 1947, have moved down the hill to this comfy bar with super cocktails and excellent nosh. The only thing missing is the view.
☎ 2140 6877 ✉ 9-13 Shelley St, Soho ☙ 11am-2am Mon-Fri, 9am-2am Sat & Sun (happy hr 5-8pm) Ⓜ Central

Sky Lounge (3, C8)
Before you can pooh-pooh the departure-lounge feel of this big, long lounge you'll have already started marvelling at the view.

Drink to remember at Groovy Mule

Happy Hour
During certain hours of the day, most pubs, bars and even certain clubs give discounts on drinks (usually one-third to one-half off) or offer a two-for-one deal.
Happy hour is usually in the late afternoon or early evening – 4pm to 8pm, say –
but the times vary widely from place to place. Depending on the season, the day of
the week and the location, some pubs' happy hours run from midday till as late as
10pm, and some resume after midnight.

Don't take flight: sit down in a scoop chair, sip a drink and scoff international snacks. ☎ 2369 1111 ✉ 18th fl, Sheraton Hong Kong Hotel & Towers, 20 Nathan Rd, Tsim Sha Tsui ⏰ 4pm-1am Mon-Fri, 2pm-2am Sat & Sun Ⓜ Tsim Sha Tsui

Staunton's Wine Bar & Cafe (6, A2)
Staunton's is swish, cool and on the ball with decent wine, a Central Escalator–cruising scene and a lovely terrace. For eats, there's light fare downstairs and a modern international restaurant above. ☎ 2973 6611 ✉ 10-12 Staunton St, Soho ⏰ 8.30am-2am midnight (happy hr 5-9pm) Ⓜ Central

V-13 Bar (6, B2)
V-13 and not V-8? The 'V' word here could only be Russian mouthwash, and there are some 80 vodkas on offer at this very cool bar, with everything from chocolate to chilli-flavoured available. The bar staff know their mixes very well. ☎ 9803 6650 ✉ 13 Old Bailey St, Soho ⏰ 5pm-midnight Mon-Thu, 5pm-late Fri, 6pm-late Sat (happy hr 5-9.30pm Mon-Fri, 6-9.30pm Sat) Ⓜ Central

CLUBS

Hong Kong has a hot and vibed-up dance club scene. Cover charges (roughly $50 to $200) sometimes include a drink and entrance can be free on particular theme nights. Special nights and parties are advertised in magazines *HK* and *bc* and online at www.hkclubbing.com.

Hostess clubs are a different kettle of fish altogether and come in two varieties here: the sleaze-pits mostly found on Peking Rd in Tsim Sha Tsui and Lockhart Rd in Wan Chai, and the more 'respectable' establishments in Tsim Sha Tsui East.

1/5 (4, F5)
Pronounced 'one-fifth', this sophisticated lounge bar and club has a broad bar backed by a two-storey drinks selec-tion from which bar staff concoct some of Hong Kong's best cocktails. It gets packed at the weekend. ☎ 2520 2515 ✉ 1st fl, Starcrest Bldg, 9 Star Street, Wan Chai ⏰ 6pm-1am Mon-Wed, 6pm-2am Thu, 6pm-3am Fri, 8pm-3am Sat (happy hr 6-9pm Mon-Fri) Ⓜ Admiralty

Bahama Mama's Caribbean Bar (3, C7)
Bahama Mama's theme is tropical isle, complete with palm trees and surfboards. It's a friendly spot and stands apart from most late-night watering holes. On Friday and Saturday nights there's a DJ and a young crowd out on the bonsai-sized dance floor. ☎ 9803 6650 ✉ 4-5 Knutsford Tce, Tsim Sha Tsui ⏰ 5pm-3am Sun-Thu, 5pm-4am Fri & Sat (happy hr 5-9pm & mid-night-late Mon-Sat, all day Sun) Ⓜ Tsim Sha Tsui

C Club (6, C3)
This fur-lined club below Lan Kwai Fong reeks of loucheness and is very

popular with its quality cocktails, sexy house music and hip-hop, velvet cushions and the double bed in the alcove.

☎ 2526 1139 ✉ Basement, California Tower, 30-32 D'Aguilar St, Central ☽ 6pm-3am Mon-Fri, 9pm-late Sat (happy hr 6-9pm Mon-Fri) Ⓜ Central

Club 97 (6, C3)

This schmoozy lounge bar has a popular happy hour (it's a gay event on Friday night) and there's reggae on Sunday. Club 97 has a 'members only' policy to turn away the underdressed, so make an effort.

☎ 2186 1897 ✉ Ground fl, Cosmos Bldg, 9-11 Lan Kwai Fong, Central ☽ 6pm-2am Mon-Thu, 6pm-4am Fri, 8pm-4am Sat & Sun (happy hr 6-9pm Mon-Fri, 8-10pm Sun) Ⓜ Central

Club Bboss (3, E7)

Hong Kong's biggest, most garish hostess bar is so overwhelming it will have you stammering. It's a ridiculous scene: chauffeured to your table in a mock Roller, extravagant floorshows, babes and men drinking Cognac by the tumbler. Bring along a well-fattened wallet.

☎ 2369 2883 ✉ Lower ground fl, New Mandarin Plaza, 14 Science Museum Rd, Tsim Sha Tsui East 💲 $450-1200 ☽ 1pm-4am Ⓜ Tsim Sha Tsui 🚌 5, 5C, 8

Club de Millennium (3, C7)

If your wallet is fat this club will most likely let you partake of its high-class giggly sleaze, where hostesses are rented by the minute and drinks are expensive. There are lavish harem-style lounges done up as Gucci, Versace and Starck showrooms.

☎ 2368 8013 ✉ 10th & 11th fl, BCC Bldg, 25-31 Carnarvon Rd (enter from Hanoi Rd), Tsim Sha Tsui 💲 from $150 ☽ 8.30pm-4am Ⓜ Tsim Sha Tsui

Club ing (7, B2)

Supremely decked-out club with chatting lounges, a long bar, popular theme nights and serious attitude. It's popular with a suave Cantonese crowd, so dress to impress. There's free entry and drinks for fashionable ladies on Thursday night.

☎ 2836 3690, 2824 0523 ✉ 4th fl, Renaissance Harbour View Hotel, 1 Harbour Rd, Wan Chai 💲 $120-160 ☽ 5pm-4am Mon-Fri, 9.30pm-4am Sat (happy hr 5pm-4am Mon & Tue, 5-8pm Wed, 5-9pm Thu & Fri) Ⓜ Wan Chai

Drop (6, A2)

Deluxe lounge action, excellent tunes and potent cocktails keep Drop strong on the scene. It's like walking into *Wallpaper* magazine, but the vibe here is unpretentiously inclusive. Members-only policy after 10pm Thursday to Saturday is (flexibly) enforced to keep the dance floor capacity at a manageable 'in like sardines' level.

☎ 2543 8856, 2543 9230 ✉ Basement, On Lok Mansion, 39-43 Hollywood Rd (enter from Cochrane St), Central ☽ 7pm-2am Mon & Tue, 7pm-3am Wed, 7pm-4am Thu, 7pm-5am Fri, 10pm-5am Sat (happy hr 7-10pm Mon-Fri) Ⓜ Central

Home (6, B2)

A meet 'n' greet for the styled and/or beautiful early on, this place turns into a bump 'n' grind later. It's one of the more popular after-hours venues and one of the few places that is still partying well after dawn in a city that *does* sleep.

☎ 2545 0023 ✉ 2nd fl, 23 Hollywood Rd, Central 💲 $100 ☽ 10pm-3am

V-13, V-vodka, V-very drunk...

Mon-Fri, 10pm-9am Sat (happy hr 10pm-midnight Mon-Sat) Ⓜ Central

Joe Banana's (7, A3)
JB's, which has been here forever (or at least since we were bopping and grooving), has dropped its long-standing wet T-shirt/boxers aesthetic and gone for more of a bamboo-bar feel. Unaccompanied females should expect a good sampler of bad pick-up lines; go with friends and have some old-fashion fun.
☎ 2529 1811 ✉ Ground fl, Shiu Lam Bldg, 23 Luard Rd, Wan Chai 💲 Wed, Fri & Sat after

11pm $100 ⏱ noon-5am Mon-Thu, noon-6am Fri & Sat, 4pm-5am Sun (happy hr 6-8pm) Ⓜ Wan Chai

Neptune Disco II (7, B3)
Neptune II is a fun club with a mostly Filipino crowd and a rockin' covers band. If everything's closing and you can't bear to stop dancing, this is definitely the place to come. It really rocks at the Sunday afternoon tea dance starting at 2pm.
☎ 2865 2238 ✉ Basement, 98-10 Jaffe Rd, Wan Chai 💲 men/women Sun $100/50 ⏱ 4pm-6am Mon-Fri, 2pm-6am Sat & Sun (happy hr 4-9pm

Mon-Fri, 2-9pm Sat) Ⓜ Wan Chai

NU (6, A1)
What was a popular post-work suit hang-out called Liquid has metamorphosed as NU, a sophisticated lounge/dance bar with live acid jazz Monday and Tuesday and DJs serving up funk, soul, R&B, house and hip-hop on other nights.
☎ 2517 3310, 2549 8386 ✉ Basement & ground fl, 1-5 Elgin St, Soho 💲 Sat $100 ⏱ 6pm-4am Sun-Fri, 8pm-6am Sat (happy hr 6-9.30pm Mon-Fri) Ⓜ Central, Sheung Wan

CINEMA

Most cinemas screen five sessions daily (around 12.30pm, 2.30pm, 5.30pm, 7.30pm and 9.30pm) with extra 4pm and 11.30pm screenings at the weekend. Almost all Chinese-language Hong Kong films have English subtitles. Admission is usually $45 to $75.

Agnès B Cinema (7, A1)
This recently renamed cinema (it was the Lim Por Yen Theatre until 2004) is *the* place for classics, revivals, alternative screenings and travelling film festivals.
☎ 2582 0200 ✉ Upper Basement, Hong Kong Arts Centre, 2 Harbour Rd, Wan Chai Ⓜ Wan Chai ♿

Broadway Cinematheque (3, B4)
An unlikely place for an alternative cinema, but it's worth checking out for new art-house releases and rerun screenings. The Kubrick Bookshop Cafe (p80) next door serves good coffee and decent pre-flick food.

☎ 2388 3188 🖥 www.cinema.com.hk ✉ Ground fl, Prosperous Garden, 3 Public Square St, Yau Ma Tei Ⓜ Yau Ma Tei ♿

Cine-Art House (7, C2)
This alternative cinema specialises in English-language films.
☎ 2827 4820 ✉ Ground fl, Sun Hung Kai Centre, 30 Harbour Rd, Wan Chai Ⓜ Wan Chai ♿

Hong Kong Film Archive (2, C2)
The place to find out what lies (or perhaps lurks) behind Hong Kong's hard-boiled film industry. The archive houses some 4300 films, runs a rich calendar

of local and foreign movie screenings and exhibits natty posters and other fine film paraphernalia. Check for screenings and times.
☎ 2739 2139, 2734 9009 (bookings) 🖥 www.filmarchive.gov.hk ✉ 50 Lei King Rd, Sai Wan Ho Ⓜ Sai Wan Ho

The Pleasure Of My Company

Fun for one is not impossible in Hong Kong. Soho in Central and Knutsford Terrace in Tsim Sha Tsui are two areas chock-a-block with laid-back bars in which you can relax. **Brecht's** (p83), **Dragon-I** (p84), **Gecko** (p85) and **Chemical Suzy** (p83) are relaxed but happening places. Lan Kwai Fong is a more highly charged pick-up zone. Wan Chai is girly-bar land and touters will assume you're on the prowl, whatever your sex.

In a business-orientated place like Hong Kong, solo dining is common. Perhaps go for food with a view (boxed text p72) so you're not stuck watching other diners watch you. At lunch time, many dim sum and noodle restaurants have tables set aside for those by themselves, so you can dine together solitarily.

JP Cinema (5, B3)
Thanks to the 'Jade Pearl' at the corner of Great George St, there's no problem finding mainstream Hollywood blockbusters in Causeway Bay. Be prepared for huge crowds at the weekend.
☎ 2881 5005 ✉ JP Plaza, 22-36 Paterson St, Causeway Bay Ⓜ Causeway Bay 🎦 yes 🚻

Palace IFC Cinema (4, D2)
This new cinema complex in the IFC Mall is arguably the most advanced and

comfortable cinematic experience in the territory.
☎ 2388 6268 ✉ Podium L1, IFC Mall, 8 Finance St, Central Ⓜ Central 🎦 yes 🚢 Star Ferry (Central) 🚻

Silvercord Cinema (3, B8)
The easy-to-find Silvercord is just along from the Star Ferry terminal. Its two theatres screen the latest Hollywood releases.
☎ 2528 8033 ✉ Ground fl, Silvercord Shopping Centre, 30 Canton Rd,

Tsim Sha Tsui Ⓜ Tsim Sha Tsui 🚢 Star Ferry (Tsim Sha Tsui) 🚻

UA Pacific Place (4, F4)
It's blessedly easy to sink into the comfort offered by one of Hong Kong's plushest cinemas. The sound system ensures you won't miss a whisper. There's also a big complex in Times Square (5, A4) above the MTR.
☎ 2869 0322 ✉ 1st fl, Pacific Place, 88 Queensway, Admiralty Ⓜ Admiralty 🎦 yes 🚻

ROCK, JAZZ & BLUES

There are usually a few decent rock bands (both local and imported) playing around town. While the Gallery at the Fringe Club is just about the only place an indie band could perform, numerous bars have house bands that play dance music. Hotel bars and clubs have Filipino bands that can play *Hotel California* and *Love is a Many-Splendored Thing* in their sleep (and yours).

Blue Door (6, B2)
This is a relaxed but very serious jazz venue with excellent music from 10.30pm to 12.30am on Saturday and good food from its Sichuanese restaurant one floor up.
☎ 2858 6555 ✉ 5th fl, Cheung Hing Commercial Bldg, 37-43 Cochrane St

(enter from Gage St), Central 💲 $80 🕐 10pm-2am Sat Ⓜ Central

Bohemian Lounge (6, B2)
This long, narrow watering hole is a great place for a libation, with live jazz Thursday after 9pm or Friday and Saturday after

10pm. Tuesday is Latino night with dance lessons.
☎ 2526 6099 ✉ 3-5 Old Bailey St, Soho 🕐 4.30-late (happy hr 5-9pm) Ⓜ Central

Chasers (3, C7)
This friendly, somewhat classy pub has a live Filipino

covers band nightly starting between 9.30pm and 10pm. Before the band cranks up, there's a jukebox to party along to and DJs after the band takes its bows. There's dancing most nights; the weekend sees a major sweat-fest.

☎ 2367 9487 ✉ Ground fl, Carlton Bldg, 2-3 Knutsford Tce, Tsim Sha Tsui ☽ 4pm-6am Mon-Fri, noon-6am Sat & Sun (happy hr 4-10pm Mon-Fri, noon-10pm Sat & Sun) Ⓜ Tsim Sha Tsui

Dusk Till Dawn (7, A3)

Live music from 10.30pm with an emphasis on beats and vibes that will get your booty shaking. The dance floor can be packed but the atmosphere is more friendly than sleazy. The food sticks to easy fillers like meat pies and burgers.

☎ 2528 4689 ✉ 76-84 Jaffe Rd, Wan Chai ☽ noon-6am Mon-Thu, noon-7am Fri & Sat, 3pm-5am Sun (happy hr 5-11pm) Ⓜ Wan Chai

Fringe Gallery (6, C3)

The Fringe, a friendly and eclectic venue on the border of the Lan Kwai Fong quadrant, has original music in its gallery/bar from 10.30pm on Friday and Saturday, with jazz, rock

Take a stand at Ned Kelly's

and world music getting the most airplay. There's a pleasant rooftop bar open in the warmer months.

☎ 2521 7251 🖳 www .hkfringe.com.hk ✉ Ground fl, Fringe Club, 2 Lower Albert Rd, Central ☽ noon-midnight Mon-Thu, noon-3am Fri & Sat (happy hr 3-9pm Mon-Thu, 3-8pm Fri & Sat Ⓜ Central (exit G)

Music Room Live (6, C3)

Nightly live rock, pop, Cuban, congo disco, R&B or funk. No cover charge makes this subdued central venue an affordable option.

☎ 2845 8477 ✉ 2nd fl, California Entertainment Bldg, 34-36 D'Aguilar St, Lan Kwai Fong ☽ 7.30pm-late (happy hr 6-9pm) Ⓜ Central

Ned Kelly's Last Stand (3, B8)

Ashley Rd in Tsim Sha Tsui has its own little time warp

in this tribute to the 19th-century Australian bush-ranger and folk hero. A great tradition continues with the Kelly Gang playing Dixieland jazz nightly from 9.30pm till 1am. Food is available and there's never a cover charge.

☎ 2376 0562 ✉ 11a Ashley Rd, Tsim Sha Tsui ☽ 11.30am-2am (happy hr 11.30am-9pm) Ⓜ Tsim Sha Tsui

Wanch (7, A3)

The Wanch has live music (mostly rock and folk) seven nights a week from 9pm, with the occasional solo guitarist thrown in. Jam night is Monday at 8pm. If you're not there for the music it can be a dubious scene – the Wanch is basically a pick-up joint.

☎ 2861 1621 ✉ 54 Jaffe Rd, Wan Chai ☽ 11am-2am Sun-Thu, 11am-4am Fri & Sat (happy hr 11am-10pm Mon-Thu, to 9pm Fri-Sun) Ⓜ Wan Chai

Cantopop

Hong Kong's home-grown popular music is known as Cantopop, a saccharine mix of romantic melodies and lyrics. Rarely radical, the songs invariably deal with such teenage concerns as unrequited love and loneliness. The music is slick and singable, thus the explosion of karaoke parlours. Big names in the music industry are thespian/crooner Andy Lau, Jackie Cheung, Faye Wong and the immortal Sally Yip, as well as more recent arrivals such as Sammi Cheung, Candy Lo, Grace Ip and Nicholas Tse.

CLASSICAL ARTS

Local classical music, dance and drama is among the best in Asia, and the schedule of foreign performances is impressive. Local theatre groups mostly perform at the Shouson Theatre of the Hong Kong Arts Centre, the Hong Kong Academy for Performing Arts, the Hong Kong Cultural Centre and the Hong Kong City Hall. Performances are usually in Cantonese, though summaries in English are often available. Smaller troupes occasionally present plays in English at the Fringe Club theatres.

**Fringe Studio & O²
Theatre (6, C3)**
These intimate theatres, each seating up to 100, host eclectic local and international performances in English and Cantonese.
☎ 2521 7251, 2521 9126 (bookings) ⌨ www.hk fringe.com.hk ✉ Ground & 1st fl, Fringe Club, 2 Lower Albert Rd, Central 💲 performances $60-250 Ⓜ Central ♿

Hong Kong Academy for Performing Arts (7, A2)
Stages local and overseas performances of dance, drama and music. The building (1985), with its striking triangular atrium and exterior Meccano-like frame, was designed by local architect Simon Kwan.
☎ 2584 8500, 2584 8514 (bookings) ⌨ www .hkapa.edu ✉ 1 Glouces-ter Rd, Wan Chai 💲 per-formances $50-700 Ⓜ Wan Chai 🎭 yes

Hong Kong Arts Centre (7, A2)
This independent contemporary arts centre showcases home-grown talent and it's Shouson Theatre hosts drama (often in English). The centre publishes a monthly listings magazine called *Artslink*. See also Pao

Galleries (p29) and Agnès B Cinema (p88).
☎ 2582 0200 ⌨ www .hkac.org.hk ✉ 2 Harbour Rd, Wan Chai 💲 performances $60-200 Ⓜ Wan Chai ♿

Hong Kong City Hall (4, E3)
Hosts classical recitals, Chinese music concerts and lots of dance. City Contemporary Dance Company is an exciting local troupe based here. Recent productions

combined dance, striptease and video, and choreographers shared the billing with fashion designers.
☎ 2921 2840, 2734 9009 (bookings) ⌨ www .cityhall.gov.hk 💲 $30-250 ✉ Lower Block, 1 Edinburgh Place, Central Ⓜ Central 🚢 Star Ferry (Central)

Hong Kong Cultural Centre (3, B9)
With two theatres and a large concert hall, this is Hong

Catch It If You Can

The best time to see and hear Chinese opera is during the **Hong Kong Arts Festival** (p82) in February or March, and outdoor performances are staged in Victoria Park during the **Mid-Autumn Festival** (p82). At other times, you might take your chances at catching a performance at the **Temple St Night Market** (p16), but the most reliable venue for opera performances year-round is the **Sunbeam Theatre** (p92) in North Point.

Chinese opera: garish and glamorous

Kong's premier performance venue. Over 850 music and opera performances annually attract more than 700,000 people. It's home to the Hong Kong Philharmonic and the Hong Kong Chinese Orchestra, and major touring companies play here.
☎ 2734 2009 ☐ www .hkculturalcentre.gov.hk

✉ 10 Salisbury Rd, Tsim Sha Tsui $ performances $100-350 Ⓜ Tsim Sha Tsui ⚓ Star Ferry (Tsim Sha Tsui) ♿

Sunbeam Theatre (2, B2)
Cantonese opera can be seen here throughout the year. Performances generally run for about a week and usually

start at about 7.30pm. The theatre is right above North Point MTR, on the northern side of King's Rd, near the intersection with Shu Kuk St.
☎ 2563 2959, 2856 0161 ✉ Kiu Fai Bldg, 423 King's Rd, North Point $ performances $60-300 Ⓜ North Point (exit A) ♿ yes

GAY & LESBIAN HONG KONG

Along with the gay and lesbian clubs and bars listed below, a few straight and mixed clubs, such as **Club 97** (p87), have gay happy hours or evenings. **GayStation** (www.gaystation.com.hk) is a monthly gay-centric listings publication available at bars and other gay venues. You might also check out the website **Gay Hong Kong** (www.gayhk.com).

Curve (6, B3)
This glitzy and innovative club with award-winning, modern décor has a mixed clientele and is less cruisey than Propaganda.
☎ 2523 0998 ✉ Ground & lower ground fl, 2 Arbuthnot Rd, Central $ $60 ☽ 8pm-3am

Mon-Thu, 8pm-late Fri & Sat (happy hr 8pm-3am Mon & Tue, 8-10pm Wed-Sat) Ⓜ Central

Propaganda (6, B2)
This is Hong Kong's premier gay dance club (and meat market). Cover charges apply on Friday and Saturday (which gets you into Works on Friday). Enter from Ezra's Lane, which runs between Pottinger and Cochrane Sts.
☎ 2868 1316 ✉ Lower ground fl, 1 Hollywood Rd, Central $ $100 Fri & Sat ☽ 9pm-4am Tue-Thu, 9pm-6am Fri & Sat (happy hr 9pm-1.30am Tue-Thu) Ⓜ Central

Rice Bar (4, B2)
This popular gay bar – it can get very crowded at the weekend – has a lounge area that sees a bit of dancing later in the night.
☎ 2851 4800 ✉ 33 Jervois St, Sheung Wan

☽ 7pm-1am Sun-Thu, 7pm-2am Fri, 8pm-3am Sat (happy hr 7-9pm Sun-Fri, 8-9pm Sat) Ⓜ Sheung Wan ♿ yes

Wally Matt Lounge (3, D7)
Cantopop karaoke and 'It's Raining Men' remixes ring throughout this boy-zone. It's dark and industrial but there are just enough seats to retreat to with a drink and watch the action.
☎ 2367 6874 ✉ 3a Granville Circuit, Tsim Sha Tsui ☽ 5pm-4am (happy hr 5-10pm) Ⓜ Tsim Sha Tsui

Works (6, C3)
Propaganda's sister club, Works is where most people start an evening on the town.
☎ 2868 6102 ✉ 1st fl, 30-32 Wyndham St, Central $ Fri & Sat $60-100 ☽ 7pm-2am (happy hr 7-9pm) Ⓜ Central

SPORTS

BADMINTON

Hong Kong Chinese are crazy about badminton and excel at it. For information about tournaments and matches, contact the **Hong Kong Badminton Association** (5, C5; ☎ 2504 8318; Rm 2005, Sports House, 1 Stadium Path, Causeway Bay).

CRICKET

The **Hong Kong International Cricket Series** is held in late October or early November. This two-day event at the Hong Kong Stadium (5, C5) sees teams from Australia, England, Hong Kong, Kenya, India, New Zealand, Pakistan, Sri Lanka and South Africa battle it out in a speedier version of the game. For information contact the **Hong Kong Cricket Association** (5, C5; ☎ 2504 8102; www.hkca.cricket.org; Rm 1019, Sports House, 1 Stadium Path, Causeway Bay).

FOOTBALL

Hong Kong has a lively amateur soccer league. Games are played on pitches inside the Happy Valley Racecourse (5, A6) and at Mong Kok Stadium (2, B1) just west of the Yuen Po St Bird Garden. Check the sports sections of the English-language papers or contact the **Hong Kong Football Association** (☎ 2712 9122; www.hkfa.com).

Find your own piece of local sport in the city's green pockets

HORSE RACING

Horse racing is Hong Kong's biggest spectator sport. There are about 80 meetings a year at the racecourses in **Happy Valley** (5, A5; p24) on Hong Kong Island and **Sha Tin** (1, D1) in New Territories. The racing season is from September to late June. Races at Happy Valley are normally held on Wednesday evenings and at Sha Tin on Saturday afternoons.

RUGBY

The **Seven-a-Side Rugby Tournament** (www.hksevens.com.hk), known as the Rugby Sevens, sees teams from all over the world come together in Hong Kong in late March for three days of lightning-fast, 15-minute matches. Even non-rugby fans scramble to get tickets, for there's also plenty of action in the stands. Matches are held at the Hong Kong Stadium (5, C5), but getting tickets isn't easy: contact the **HKTB** (p119) or **Hong Kong Rugby Football Union** (5, C5; ☎ 2504 8311; www.hkrugby.com; Rm 2001, Sports House, 1 Stadium Path, Causeway Bay).

Sleeping

With the exception of some swooningly lovely landmark deluxe properties, Hong Kong's hotels tend to impress only with their numbing sameness or, at the bottom end, with their resemblance to dank (or worse) cupboards. But with some 510 hotels and other forms of accommodation containing almost 43,000 rooms and occupancy between 70% and 80% (depending on the season), you should find a suitable temporary abode.

Hong Kong's two high seasons are from March to April and October to November, though things can be tight around Chinese New Year (late January or February) as well. Outside these periods, rates drop (sometimes substantially) and little extras can come your way: airport transport, room upgrades, late checkout, free breakfast and complimentary cocktails. If the hotel seems a bit quiet when you arrive, it might be worth asking for an upgrade.

Hong Kong's deluxe hotels are special places, with individual qualities that propel them above the rest. Expect discreet, smooth-as-silk service, large bathtubs, superlative climate control, extensive cable TV, and Internet access, dataports and fax machines.

Top-end hotels are in spiffy locations: they also have smart, comfortable rooms with excellent air-con, in-house movies and a good variety of room service options. Amenities include business facilities, bars and restaurants and fluent English-speaking staff.

Mid-range hotels tend to be generic business/tourist establishments with little to distinguish one from another. Rooms are spacious enough and usually have a bath, limited cable TV and room service.

The majority of Hong Kong's budget digs are in Kowloon, with many on or near Nathan Rd. Though most budget rooms are very small, the places listed here are clean and cheerily shabby rather than grim and grimy.

The hotels included in this chapter all have at the very least private bathrooms, telephones, TVs and air-conditioning.

Room Rates

The following categories indicate the cost per night of a standard double room; be aware that most places will add 3% government tax and a 10% service charge to their quoted rates.

Deluxe	$3000 and over
Top End	$1600-3000
Mid-Range	$700-1600
Budget	$700 and under

DELUXE

Grand Hyatt Hotel (7, A1)
This hotel is among the most sumptuous in town yet still technologically up to date. Each of its 572 rooms is charged with cyber-concierge and Internet access and most have a harbour view.

☎ 2588 1234 💻 http:// hongkong.hyatt.com ✉ 1 Harbour Rd, Wan Chai Ⓜ Wan Chai ♿ good (3 rooms) 🚭

Hotel InterContinental Hong Kong (3, C9)
This 514-room hotel, which boasts the finest waterfront position in the territory, tilts at modernity while bowing to colonial traditions, such as its fleet of Rolls Royce's, uniformed doormen and incessant brass-polishing. The impeccable service ensures a lot of repeat custom.

Baby Boons

Business travellers and tourists alike are bringing their children in increasing numbers to Hong Kong, and many deluxe and top-end hotels – including the Peninsula Hong Kong, the Island Shangri-La and the Mandarin Oriental – have special programs for children, ranging from art workshops to Chinese cookery lessons. Check with individual hotels for services they offer their young guests.

☎ 2721 1211
🖥 www.hongkong-ic.intercontinental.com
✉ 18 Salisbury Rd, Tsim Sha Tsui Ⓜ Tsim Sha Tsui ⛴ Star Ferry (Tsim Sha Tsui) ♿ good (2 rooms) ✕ Yü (p72) ♨

Mandarin Oriental Hotel (4, D3)

Hong Kong Island counterpart to the Peninsula Hong Kong (p19), the 541-room Mandarin is not architecturally as impressive but has a healthy dose of old-world charm. Styling is subdued, and the service, food and atmosphere are stellar.
☎ 2522 0111 🖥 www.mandarinoriental.com ✉ 5 Connaught Rd,

Central Ⓜ Central ⛴ Star Ferry (Central) 🐶 Yes ♿ fair ✕ Vong (p69), Cafe (p67) ♨

Peninsula Hong Kong (3, C8)

Lording over the southern tip of Kowloon, Hong Kong's finest hotel (see also p19) evokes colonial elegance, but its 300 guestrooms are as modern as any other hotels, with Internet access, fax machines and CD and DVD players. Rooms in the newer wing offer spectacular harbour views.
☎ 2920 2888 🖥 www.peninsula.com ✉ Salisbury Rd, Tsim Sha Tsui Ⓜ Tsim Sha Tsui ⛴ Star Ferry (Tsim Sha Tsui)

♿ good (3 rooms) ✕ Felix (p77), Spring Moon (p78) ♨

Ritz-Carlton Hong Kong (4, D3)

This is a truly beautiful hotel with 245 plush rooms and suites that manage to be cosy and incredibly distinguished at the same time. Views from harbourside rooms are breathtaking, but the best views might be from the pool: lie back and soak up the skyline.
☎ 2877 6666 🖥 www.ritzcarlton.com ✉ 3 Connaught Rd, Central Ⓜ Central ⛴ Star Ferry (Central) 🐶 Yes ♿ good (2 rooms) ♨

The Royal Plaza Hotel (p99) sprouts out of a Mong Kok shopping centre

TOP END

Conrad Hong Kong (4, E5)

This elegant but unstuffy 513-room hotel above Pacific Place gets enthusiastic reviews for its attention to business travellers' needs. Its foyer bar/lounge is a gossipy, corporate hang-out.

☎ 2521 3838 ▫ www .conradhotels.com ✉ Pacific Place, 88 Queensway, Admiralty Ⓜ Admiralty ⓘ Yes ♿ good (2 rooms) ⚑

Excelsior Hong Kong (5, B3)

Part of the Mandarin Oriental Group and a Causeway Bay landmark, this 884-room hotel offers fabulous harbour views and convenient shopping. With all the shops in the area, however, the lobby is always a bit of a madhouse.

☎ 2894 8888 ▫ www .excelsiorhongkong.com ✉ 281 Gloucester Rd, Causeway Bay Ⓜ Causeway Bay ♿ good (2 rooms) ⚑

Hyatt Regency (3, C8)

The towering 723-room Hyatt, on the 'wrong' side of Nathan Rd, is slightly lower priced than most of its top-end neighbours and is a relaxed kind of hotel. Its Chinese Restaurant is justly revered.

☎ 2311 1234 ▫ http:// hongkong.hyatt.com ✉ 67 Nathan Rd, Tsim Sha Tsui Ⓜ Tsim Sha Tsui ♿ good (2 rooms) ✕ Chinese Restaurant (p76) ⚑

Island Shangri-La Hong Kong (4, E4)

The 56-storey Shangri-La's sterile exterior conceals its swish sophistication; its 565 guestrooms are among the loveliest in Hong Kong. Atrium bubble lifts link the 39th and 56th floors; facilities include an outdoor spa and a 24-hour gym.

☎ 2877 3838 ▫ www .shangri-la.com ✉ Pacific Place, Supreme Court Rd, Admiralty Ⓜ Admiralty ⓘ Yes ♿ excellent (6 rooms) ✕ Petrus (p73) ⚑

JW Marriot Hong Kong (4, F4)

Though focused on business travellers (that would explain the almost daily fluctuations in room rates), this 602-room hotel is also popular with shopaholics, who can feed their addiction downstairs at Pacific Place. The heated outdoor swimming pool is a verdant oasis.

☎ 2810 8366 ▫ www .marriotthotels.com ✉ Pacific Place, 88 Queensway, Admiralty Ⓜ Admiralty ⓘ Yes ♿ good (4 rooms) ⚑

Marco Polo Hong Kong (3, B8)

The lynchpin in the Marco Polo Hotel group's Canton Rd trio of hotels, this 665-room property is the closest to the Star Ferry and has plenty of shopping in the attached Harbour City shopping mall (p59).

☎ 2113 0888 ▫ www .marcopolohotels.com ✉ Harbour City, 3 Canton Rd, Tsim Sha Tsui Ⓜ Tsim Sha Tsui ⛴ Star Ferry (Tsim Sha Tsui) ⚑

Renaissance Harbour View Hotel (7, B2)

This spectacular 860-room hotel adjoins the almost-in-the-water Convention and Exhibition Centre, ensuring

Please allow me: the Renaissance Hotel doorman

Special Deals

The best rates at the better hotels tend to be available through travel agents and booking services. Check flight/accommodation packages in advance or visit the **Hong Kong Hotels Association** (☎ 2383 8380; www.hkha.com.hk) desk at the airport on arrival. For mid-range and top-end discounted rates try a hotel room consolidator such as **Phoenix Services Agency** (☎ 2722 7378; info@phoenixtrvl .com) or **Traveller Services** (☎ 2375 2222; www.taketraveller.com).

steady suit-and-tie custom and harbour views from 65% of the guestrooms. Leisure travellers will appreciate informed concierges and the enormous outdoor pool overlooking the harbour. There is a kiddies' pool too. ☎ 2802 8888 🖳 http://marriott.com/property /propertypage/hkghv ✉ 1 Harbour Rd, Wan Chai Ⓜ Wan Chai 🚢 Star Ferry (Wan Chai) ♿ good (2 rooms) 🍴 Dynasty (p73) ⚄

Royal Garden (3, D7)

This often overlooked 442-room property is one of the best-equipped hotels on Kowloon side and one of Hong Kong's most attractive accommodation options overall. From the chic blonde wood and chrome lobby to the rooftop sports complex (25m pool, putting green and tennis court with million dollar views), the Royal Garden kicks ass. ☎ 2721 5215 🖳 www .rghk.com.hk ✉ 69 Mody Rd, Tsim Sha Tsui East 🚌 5C, 8 (from Star Ferry pier) 🚢 Tsim Sha Tsui East Ferry Pier Ⓜ Tsim Sha Tsui ♿ excellent (7 rooms) 🍴 Sabatini (p78) ⚄

Sheraton Hong Kong Hotel & Towers (3, C9)

This very American hostelry (the ground floor is the 1st floor, escalators travel on the right) at the start of Nathan Rd is as central as you'll find in Tsim Sha Tsui. Rooms in the towers offer better harbour views than those in the hotel. The Sky Lounge (p85) on the 18th floor is worth a visit for its

Dizzying grandeur of the Peninsula (p95)

stunning harbour views. ☎ 2369 1111 🖳 http://www.starwoodhotels .com/sheraton/index/html ✉ 20 Nathan Rd, Tsim Sha Tsui Ⓜ Tsim Sha Tsui ♿ excellent (12 rooms) ⚄

MID-RANGE

Charterhouse Hotel (4, J4)

This hotel on the leafy side of Wan Chai is a pretty good deal with almost top-end rooms for mid-range rates. ☎ 2833 5566 🖳 www .charterhouse.com ✉ 209-219 Wan Chai Rd, Wan Chai Ⓜ Wan Chai 🅿 Yes ♿ excellent (5 rooms) ⚄

Dorsett Seaview Hotel (3, B4)

The 257 rooms at this hotel, which does a big trade in mainland Chinese tour groups, are fine, but not so delightful that they'll keep you inside: the Temple St Night Market and the shops of Nathan Rd are within easy reach and the Tin Hau Temple is practically at the

hotel's front door. ☎ 2782 0882 🖳 www .dorsettseaview.com.hk ✉ 268 Shanghai St, Yau Ma Tei Ⓜ Yau Ma Tei ♿ good (3 rooms) ⚄

Empire Hotel Kowloon (3, D7)

The chic Kowloon branch of the Empire chain houses state-of-the-art technical

A room with a view

features, 'exciting' bath-rooms, 'trendy excellent restaurants' and a truly magnificent indoor atrium swimming pool and spa. It's an easy stroll from here to just about anywhere in what locals call 'Tsimsy'.
☎ 2685 3000
🖥 www.asiastandard.com ✉ 62 Kimberley Rd, Tsim Sha Tsui Ⓜ Tsim Sha Tsui ♿ excellent (13 rooms) 🧍

Harbour View International House (7, A2)
Right next door to the Hong Kong Arts Centre and a mere stroll to the Hong Kong Convention & Exhibition Centre and Wan Chai ferry terminal, this YMCA-run 320-room hotel is excellent value for its lo-cation. Most of the Harbour View is simply furnished but perfectly adequate rooms look out over the harbour.
☎ 2802 0111 🖥 www.harbour.ymca.org.hk ✉ 4 Harbour Rd, Wan Chai Ⓜ Wan Chai 🚢 Star Ferry (Wan Chai) 🧍

Holiday Inn Golden Mile (3, C8)
The 600 guestrooms at this place are reliably good and

you've got the schmoozy Hari's bar (p85) on site.
☎ 2369 3111 🖥 www.goldenmile-hk.holiday-inn.com ✉ 50 Nathan Rd, Tsim Sha Tsui Ⓜ Tsim Sha Tsui ♿ good (1 room) 🧍

Kimberley Hotel (3, C7)
This 546-room hotel is one of the better mid-range hotels in Tsim Sha Tsui, with assured staff and good rooms and facilities (includ-ing golf nets).
☎ 2723 3888 🖥 www.kimberleyhotel.com.hk ✉ 28 Kimberley Rd, Tsim Sha Tsui Ⓜ Tsim Sha Tsui ♿ good (3 rooms) 🧍

Kowloon Hotel (3, C8)
Part of the Peninsula Hotel group, the 736-room Kowloon Hotel has an 'also ran' feel about it but is popular for its unflappable service, decent rooms and wonderful Wan Loong Court restaurant in the basement that serves up great dim sum.
☎ 2929 2888 🖥 www.thekowloonhotel.com ✉ 19-21 Nathan Rd, Tsim Sha Tsui Ⓜ Tsim Sha Tsui 🚢 Star Ferry (Tsim Sha Tsui) 🍴 Wan Loong Court (p79) 🧍

Luk Kwok Hotel (7, B3)
This is a relatively small (196 rooms), no-frills, no harbour views kinda place (though it talks up its city and mountain aspects). However staff are keen and helpful and you're close to the bustle of Wan Chai.
☎ 2866 2166 🖥 www.lukkwokhotel.com ✉ 72 Gloucester Rd, Wan Chai Ⓜ Wan Chai ♿ good (2 rooms) 🧍

Miramar Hotel (3, C7)
This 525-room landmark is central and convenient to the Miramar Shopping Cen-tre over Kimberley Rd. It has some fine outlets, including the restaurant Dong.
☎ 2368 1111 🖥 www.miramarhk.com ✉ 118-130 Nathan Rd, Tsim Sha Tsui ♿ fair 🍴 Dong (p77) 🧍

Park Hotel (3, D7)
Ongoing renovations at this 430-room hotel has seen standards (and prices) go up. The history and science museums are over the road and the Granville Rd shop-ping strip a block away. Enter from Cameron Rd.
☎ 2366 1371 🖥 www.parkhotel.com.hk ✉ 61-65 Chatham Rd Sth, Tsim Sha Tsui Ⓜ Tsim Sha Tsui ♿ good (2 rooms) 🧍

Rosedale on the Park (5, C4)
This Best Western property touts itself as Hong Kong's first 'cyber boutique hotel'. It's a bit big for a boutique but its 274 rooms are attractively appointed and its location opposite Victoria Park is excellent.

☎ 2127 8606 🖳 www
.rosedale.com.hk ✉ 8
Shelter St Ⓜ Causeway
Bay 🈶 Yes ♿ good (3
rooms) ⛎

Royal Pacific Hotel & Towers (3, B7)

The rooms – some 675 in
total – are more expensive
in the harbour-facing tower
than in the hotel. There's
a walkway to Kowloon
Park, leading on to Nathan
Rd and the Tsim Sha Tsui
MTR station; the hotel is
connected to the China ferry
terminal.
☎ 2736 1188 🖳 www
.royalpacific.com.hk
✉ 33 Canton Rd, Tsim
Sha Tsui Ⓜ Tsim Sha
Tsui ⚓ Star Ferry (Tsim
Sha Tsui) ♿ excellent
(6 rooms) ⛎

Royal Plaza Hotel (2, B1)

The plushness is a bit
overdone, but the 469-room
Plaza is comfortable and
the bird and flower markets
are just on the other side
of Prince Edward Rd. The
heated no-steam bath-
room mirrors are a stroke
of genius and the large
outdoor pool is a lounge
lizard's nirvana.
☎ 2928 8822 🖳 www
.royalplaza.com.hk
✉ 193 Prince Edward Rd
West, Mong Kok Ⓜ Prince
Edward 🚆 Mong Kok KCR
East Rail ⛎

Stanford Hillview Hotel (3, D6)

This 170-room hotel is
one of our favourites, set
back from Nathan Rd in a
quiet, leafy little corner of

Tsim Sha Tsui but close to
the food, fun and frolick-
ing of Knutsford Terrace
(from where you enter the
lobby).
☎ 2722 7822 🖳 www
.stanfordhillview.com
✉ 13-17 Observatory
Rd, Tsim Sha Tsui Ⓜ Tsim
Sha Tsui ♿ good (2
rooms) ⛎

Wharney Hotel Hong Kong (7, A3)

Noteworthy for its rooftop
swimming pool and outdoor
whirlpool, the 358-room
Wharney is a mid-range
option in the heart of Wan
Chai with good long-stay
packages.
☎ 2861 1000 🖳 www
.wharney.com ✉ 57-73
Lockhart Rd, Wan Chai
Ⓜ Wan Chai ⛎

BUDGET

The Shamrock offers
budget bliss

Bishop Lei International House (4, B4)

This 203-room hotel isn't
luxurious but it is central
and it has a swimming pool
and gym. The Zoological &
Botanical Gardens are an
amble away.
☎ 2868 0828 🖳 www
.bishopleihtl.com.hk ✉ 4
Robinson Rd, Mid-Levels
🚌 3B, 12, 12M ♿ good
(2 rooms)

Booth Lodge (3, C3)

Run by the Salvation
Army, this 54-room place
is appropriately spartan,
but clean and comfortable.
Rates include breakfast.
☎ 2771 9266 🖳 http://
boothlodge.salvation.org
.hk ✉ 11 Wing Sing Lane,
Yau Ma Tei Ⓜ Yau Ma Tei

BP International House (3, B6)

This recently renovated
535-room hotel, owned
by the Scout Association
of Hong Kong, overlooks
Kowloon Park and is a short
walk to Nathan Rd and the
Jordan MTR. Some rooms
have bunk beds, making
this a good option if you're
travelling with kids.
☎ 2378 7611 🖳 www
.bpih.com.hk ✉ 8
Austin Rd, Tsim Sha Tsui
Ⓜ Jordan ♿ excellent
(11 rooms) ⛎

Caritas Bianchi Lodge (3, C3)

This 90-room hotel-
cum-guesthouse is run by
a Catholic social welfare
organisation and has

straightforward, fairly spacious rooms. Though it's just off Nathan Rd the rear rooms are very quiet.

☎ 2388 1111
💻 cblresv@bianchi-lodge.com ✉ 4 Cliff Rd, Yau Ma Tei Ⓜ Yau Ma Tei ♿

Garden View International House (4, C5)

Straddling the border of Central and the Mid-Levels, the YWCA-run Garden View (133 rooms) overlooks the lush Hong Kong Zoological & Botanical Gardens. Accommodation is plain but comfortable; it's the only place in the area that falls outside the deluxe or top-end categories.

☎ 2877 3737 💻 www
.ywca.org.hk ✉ 1 MacDonnell Rd, Central
🚌 3B, 12, 12M, minibus 1A ♿ good (2 rooms)

Ice House (6, C3)

In terms of location, Ice House offers one of the coolest deals in Central. Spread over 13 floors, it has 64 standard and superior open-plan 'suites' with a kitchenette and work desk with Internet access. It's become a favourite of visiting hacks, who feed and water at the Foreign Correspondents' Club next door.

☎ 2836 7333 💻 www
.icehouse.com.hk ✉ 38 Ice House St, Central
🚌 13, 23A, 26

Rent-a-Room Hong Kong (3, C5)

This great place has 40 immaculate rooms in a block of flats around the corner from the Jordan MTR station. Each room has shower, TV, telephone (no charge for local calls), Internet access and a fridge.

☎ 2366 3011, 9023 8022
💻 www.rentaroomhk
.com ✉ Flat A, 2nd fl, Knight Garden, 7-8 Tak Hing St, Yau Ma Tei
Ⓜ Jordan ♿

Salisbury (3, C8)

Book a room at this YMCA-run hotel and you'll be rewarded with professional service and excellent fitness facilities. The 365 rooms are comfortable but basic; you won't notice if you keep your eyes on the harbour view. There are family rooms and four-bed dorms.

☎ 2268 7888 💻 www
.ymcahk.org.hk ✉ 41 Salisbury Rd, Tsim Sha Tsui Ⓜ Tsim Sha Tsui
⛴ Star Ferry (Tsim Sha Tsui) 🍴 Salisbury Dining Room (p78) ♿ good (4 rooms) ♿

Shamrock Hotel (3, C6)

The Shamrock offers fantastic value for its category and location, with 158 well-sized, clean and airy guestrooms. Jordan MTR is just outside the front door.

☎ 2735 2271 💻 www
.shamrockhotel.com.hk
✉ 223 Nathan Rd, Yau Ma Tei Ⓜ Jordan ♿

Wesley (4, F4)

This central, 22-storey property with 251 rooms offers one of the better deals on Hong Kong Island, but there are very few facilities and the service is cavalier at best. Rates depend on the size of the room.

☎ 2866 6688 💻 www
.hanglung.com ✉ 22 Hennessy Rd, Wan Chai
Ⓜ Admiralty 🚗 Yes

For a Longer Stay

Those staying in Hong Kong for a longer period may be interested in serviced apartments, a mostly post-colonial innovation that is becoming more common, particularly in and around Central. Some hotels listed in this chapter, including **Ice House** (left) in Central, the **Wesley** (above) and **Wharney** (p99) in Wan Chai and **Bishop Lei** (p99) in the Mid-Levels, offer extraordinarily good value long-term packages. Several properties owned by **Hanlun Habitats** (4, B4; ☎ 2868 0168; www.hanlunhabitats.com) are within striking distance of each other in Mid-Levels and are accessible via the Central Escalator; these are among the nicest serviced apartments available. Prices range from $16,500 to $28,000 per month.

About Hong Kong

HISTORY

Before the arrival of the British, Hong Kong was a neglected corner of the Qing dynasty (1644–1911) empire inhabited by farmers, fishermen and pirates. Trade between China and Britain began around 1685, but the balance was unfavourable to the Europeans – until they began running opium into China in the late 18th century.

Despite bans issued by Chinese Emperor Jia Qin and his son and successor, Dao Guang, trade in opium continued until 1839 when the commissioner of Guangzhou, Lin Zexu, destroyed 20,000 chests of the 'foreign mud'. This gave Britain the pretext they needed for military action against China. British gunboats blockaded Guangzhou and then sailed north, forcing the Chinese to negotiate. Captain Charles Elliot, the chief superintendent of trade, demanded that a small, hilly island near the mouth of the Pearl River be ceded 'in perpetuity'. Hong Kong formally became a British possession in August 1842.

The so-called Second Anglo-Chinese War (1856–60) gave the British the Kowloon peninsula, and less than 40 years later they gained the much larger 'New Territories'. Instead of annexing the land outright, however, the two parties agreed to a 99-year lease.

Steady numbers of Chinese refugees fleeing war and famine entered the colony during the 1920s and '30s; in 1941 Japanese forces swept down from Guangzhou and occupied the territory for four years.

The communist revolution in 1949 sent more refugees pouring into Hong Kong. On a paltry, war-ravaged foundation, both local and foreign businesses built an immense manufacturing (notably textiles and garments) and financial services centre that transformed Hong Kong into one of the world's great economic success stories. By 1960, Hong Kong was home to about 3 million people, up from a population of 600,000 at the end of the war.

China, having locked itself in its own cage in the 1950s, began rattling it in the next decade. In 1967, at the height of the so-called Cultural

Mao's Red Army memorabilia in the Cat Street curio shops

Land Grab Gag

'Albert is so amused at my having got the island of Hong Kong' wrote the usually purse-lipped Victoria to King Leopold of Belgium in 1841. While the queen's consort may have seen the funny side of her owning a lump of rock off the southern coast of China, Lord Palmerston was not so entertained. 'A barren island with hardly a house upon it! It will never be a mart for trade', he raged in a letter to Charles Elliot and relieved the captain of his post.

Revolution, riots provoked by the ultra-leftist Red Guards rocked the colony. Panic spread but Hong Kong stood firm; Chinese Premier Chou Enlai intervened and Hong Kong got on with the business of making money.

Few people gave much thought to Hong Kong's future until the early 1980s, when the British and Chinese governments started meeting to decide what would happen after 30 June 1997. Though Britain was legally bound to hand back only the New Territories, most of the population lived in the New Territories and it would have been an untenable division. In December 1984 Britain formally agreed to hand back the entire territory, and a joint declaration allowed the 'Hong Kong Special Administrative Region (SAR) of China' to retain its social, economic and legal systems for 50 years after the handover. The Chinese catch phrase for this was 'One country, two systems'. In 1988 Beijing published the Basic Law for Hong Kong, which enshrined rights to property, travel, trade and free speech.

Nervousness increased as the handover date drew closer, especially after 1989 when Chinese troops mowed down pro-democracy demonstrators in Beijing's Tiananmen Square, and both people and capital moved to safe havens overseas. A belated attempt by Britain to increase the number of democratically elected members of Hong Kong's Legislative Council spurred China to set up a pro-Beijing Provisional Legislative Council across the border in Shenzhen. On 1 July 1997 this body took office in Hong Kong, and Shanghai-born shipping magnate and big FOC (friend of China), Tung Chee Hwa (1937–), was named chief executive. He was returned for a second five-year term in March 2002.

Hong Kong has weathered many storms since the handover. The one that caused the greatest damage to the credibility of the SAR administration came in 1999 when the government, with Beijing's assistance, overturned a high court ruling allowing residency rights for the China-born offspring of parents who became Hong Kong citizens after 1997. Since then there has been a severe economic downturn, several outbreaks of Severe Acute Respiratory Syndrome (SARS)

The right of assembly is guaranteed by law

which led to the deaths of hundreds of people, and a number of other crucial interventions by Chinese authorities in Hong Kong's affairs. Clearly Hong Kong is not as autonomous as its name suggests.

ENVIRONMENT

Pollution has been and remains a problem in Hong Kong, but it wasn't until 1989, with the formation of the Environmental Protection Department (EPD), that government authorities acted decisively to clean up the mess. The EPD has had to deal with decades of serious environmental abuse and – almost as serious – a population that until recently didn't know (or care) about the implications of littering and pollution.

Hong Kong's waterways and air are in a terrible state, but there have been some slight improvements over the past decade. A new disposal system is now collecting up to 70% of the sewage entering Victoria Harbour and the *E.coli* count indicating the presence of sewage has stabilised. At the same time the Hong Kong and Guangdong provincial governments have announced a joint intent to reduce regional emissions of sulphur dioxide, nitrogen oxides, breathable suspended particulates and volatile organic compounds by more than half by 2010. Other positive signs include levying on-the-spot fines for spitting and littering, monitoring almost three dozen gazetted beaches for disease-causing bacteria and introducing more recycling bins. However, these are minor initiatives given the 17,500 tonnes of domestic, industrial and construction waste generated in Hong Kong daily.

Where the Grass is Greener

Not all of Hong Kong is ravaged. Some 38% of the total land area has been designated as protected country parkland. These 23 parks – for the most part in the New Territories and on the Outlying Islands, but also encompassing the slopes of Hong Kong Island – comprise uplands, woodlands, coastlines, marshes and all of Hong Kong's 17 freshwater reservoirs. In addition, there are four protected marine parks and one marine reserve.

GOVERNMENT & POLITICS

Hong Kong 'constitution' is the Basic Law, which in theory bestows freedom on Hong Kong in everything except foreign affairs. But Hong Kong does not have what could be called a democratic system, although democratic elements exist within its structure. In effect, business governs the territory,

Hong Kong's skyline: a jumble of board-rooms and bedrooms

the democratic elements that do exist are limited and the people are, to a large degree, apolitical.

The executive branch of power is led by the chief executive. He or she selects an Executive Council, which serves as a cabinet and advises on policy matters. The top three slots are the chief secretary for the administration of government; the financial secretary, responsible for the economic policies of the government; and the secretary for justice, charged with drafting legislation.

The Legislative Council debates and passes legislation proposed by the Executive Council and approves public expenditure. An independent judiciary headed by a chief justice administers justice and interprets the law.

Since 1997 the Hong Kong government has become more executive-led, turning the Legislative Council into little more than a rubber-stamp body. Furthermore, the civil service is less accountable, prompting fears that the corruption that dogged it in the past will return.

ECONOMY

Business is Hong Kong's heart and soul. Despite monopolies in certain sections of the economy (eg transport and power generation), the territory remains a capitalist's dream, with virtually unrestricted trade, a hard-working labour force, excellent telecommunications and very low taxes. The maximum personal income tax is 16%; company profits tax is capped at 17.5%.

Did You Know?

- Hong Kong's annual per capita GDP of US$28,700 exceeds that of Japan and most EU countries.
- The Kwun Tong District in Kowloon is the most densely populated place on earth, with more than 50,000 people per sq km.
- Hong Kong consumes more oranges than any other place on earth.
- Hong Kong welcomed some 15.5 million visitors in 2003, half of them from the mainland.
- The territory has the world's highest per-capita consumption of cognac, accounting for more than 10% of the worldwide market.
- Prime office space in Central rents for between $375 (Two IFC) and $485 (Cheung Kong Centre) per sq metre.

Service industries employ about 85% of Hong Kong's workforce and make up nearly 87.5% of its GDP. China is by far Hong Kong's largest trading partner, supplying a third of the territory's total imports and exports. Japan, Taiwan, the USA, Singapore and the European Union follow.

The early 21st century was a trying time for the Hong Kong economy. Hong Kong maintained an average GDP growth of 5% through the 1990s and peaked at 10% in 2000, but fell to just 0.6% in 2001. Three years later a surge in trade with China and a phenomenal increase of visitors from the mainland saw consumer prices rise (and deflation disappear) for the first time in almost six years. Unemployment fell to a two-year low of 6.9%, and a confident government was predicting a growth of between 6% and 7.5%. For the visitor, that translates as higher prices.

SOCIETY & CULTURE

While Hong Kong may seem very Westernised, Chinese beliefs and traditions persist. Buddhism and Taoism – mixed with elements of Confucianism, traditional ancestor worship and animism – are the dominant religions. In general, though, Chinese people are much less concerned with high-minded philosophies than they are with the pursuit of worldly success, the appeasement of spirits and predicting the future. Visits to temples are usually made to ask the gods favours for specific things, such as a loved one's health or the success of a business.

Prayer flags to the Sea Goddess blowing in the wind

Feng Shui

Literally 'wind water', feng shui aims to balance the elements of nature to create a harmonious environment. It's been in practice since the 12th century, and continues to influence the design of buildings, highways, parks, tunnels and grave sites in Hong Kong. To guard against evil spirits, who can move only in straight lines, doors are often positioned at an angle. For similar reasons, beds cannot face doorways. Ideally, homes and businesses should have a view of calm water (even a fish tank helps). Corporate heads shouldn't have offices that face west: otherwise profits will go in the same direction as the setting sun.

Fortune-Telling

There are any number of props and implements that Chinese use to predict the future but the most common method of divination in Hong Kong are the 'fortune sticks' (p36) found at Buddhist and Taoist temples.

T'ai Chi

Short for *taijiquan* (or 'fist of the supreme ultimate'), this slow-motion martial art has been popular for centuries, especially among older people. The movements develop breathing muscles, promote digestion and improve muscle tone and can also form a solid foundation for any other martial arts practice.

Zodiac

As in the Western system of astrology, the Chinese zodiac has 12 signs, but their representations are all animals. Your sign is based on the year of your birth (according to the lunar calendar). Being born or married in a particular year is

The Year of the...
- Rooster (2005)
- Dog (2006)
- Pig (2007)
- Rat (2008)
- Ox (2009)
- Tiger (2010)

believed to determine one's fortune, so parents often plan for their children's sign. The year of the dragon sees the biggest jump in the birth rate, closely followed by the year of the tiger.

ARTS

The phrase 'cultural desert' can no longer be used for Hong Kong. There are Western and Chinese orchestras, dance troupes and several theatre companies, and the number of international arts festivals seems to grow each year. See p81 for listings and venue information.

Architecture

Architecture enthusiasts will find Hong Kong Island's Central and Wan Chai districts a fascinating showcase for the modern and contemporary. The **Bank of China Tower** (p18), **Hongkong & Shanghai Bank** (p31), **Lippo Centre** (4, E4), **Hong Kong Convention and Exhibition Centre** (p31), **Two IFC** (boxed text p31) and the **Center** (p31) are all impressive in their own way and very photogenic.

However progress has been made at the expense of history. Among the few examples of pre-colonial Chinese architecture left in urban Hong

May the twain never meet: the Lippo Centre's unique geometry

Kong are **Tin Hau Temple** (5, C3) near Causeway Bay and the village house at the **Law Uk Folk Museum** (p28). There are temples and walled villages in the New Territories and Kowloon, including **Kowloon Walled City Park** (p34).

Colonial architecture is also in short supply. Some remaining examples include the **Legislative Council Building** (p32) and **Murray House** (boxed text p45).

Do Dos & No Nos

There aren't many unusual rules of etiquette to follow in Hong Kong; in general, common sense will take you as far as you'll need to go. But on matters of identity, appearance, gift-giving and the big neighbour to the north, local people might see things a little differently to you. For pointers on how to conduct yourself at the table, see p65.

- **Clothing** Beyond the suited realm of business, smart casual dress is acceptable even at swish restaurants, but save your bikini for the beach and keep your flip-flops at the hotel. On the beach topless is a local turnoff and nudity a no-no.
- **Cards** Hong Kong is name-card crazy and in business circles they are a must. People simply won't take you seriously unless you have one (be sure to offer it with *both* hands). Bilingual cards can usually be printed within 24 hours; try printers along Man Wa Lane in Central or ask your hotel to direct you.
- **China** Don't diss it, you're in it (and everyone knows all about the mainland's successes and failures anyway).
- **Colours** Colours are symbolic to the Chinese. Red symbolises good luck, virtue and wealth (though writing in red can convey anger or unfriendliness). White symbolises death, so avoid giving white flowers (except at funerals).
- **Face** Think status and respect (both receiving and showing): keep your cool, be polite, and order a glass of vintage Champagne or XO brandy at the Pen or Mandarin for $500.
- **Gifts** If you want to give flowers, chocolates or wine to someone (a fine idea if invited to their home) they may appear reluctant for fear of seeming greedy, but insist and they'll give in. Money enclosed in little red envelopes called *laisee* is given at weddings and the lunar new year.

Chinese Opera

Chinese opera is a world away from the Western variety. It is a mixture of singing, dialogue, mime, acrobatics and dancing that foreigners may find hard to appreciate. Performances can last up to five or six hours, and the audience makes an evening of it – eating, chatting among themselves and changing seats when bored, laughing at the funny parts, crying at the sad bits.

Costumes, props and body language reveal much of the meaning in Chinese opera – check out the enlightening display on Cantonese opera at the **Hong Kong Heritage Museum** (p26). For a better understanding of this art form join the Cantonese Opera Appreciation Class in the 'Meet the People' program (boxed text p45).

Dance

Hong Kong's professional dance companies are the Hong Kong Dance Company (Chinese traditional and folk); City Contemporary Dance Company (modern); and Hong Kong Ballet (classical and contemporary). See p91 for details.

One Chinese tradition that lives on in Hong Kong is the lion dance. A dance troupe under an elaborately painted Chinese lion costume leaps around to the sound of clanging cymbals, giving the dancers a chance to demonstrate their acrobatic skills.

Music

Classical music is alive and well in Hong Kong. The city boasts Chinese, philharmonic and chamber orchestras and a sinfonietta. Established overseas performers frequently make it to Hong Kong, especially during February's Hong Kong Arts Festival (see the boxed text p82).

Cantopop dominates the popular music scene in Hong Kong; see the boxed text p90.

Painting

Painting in Hong Kong falls into three broad categories: contemporary local, classical Chinese and classical Western. Contemporary local art differs from that of mainland China, as Hong Kong artists are largely the offspring of refugees and the products of cultural fusion; they blend East and West and are concerned with finding their orientation in the metropolis through personal statement. The best places to see examples of this art are the **Hong Kong Museum of Art** (p26), **Hanart TZ Gallery** (p29) and **Para/Site Art Space** (p30).

Theatre

Nearly all theatre here is Western in form but is staged in Cantonese. Theatre groups include the **Hong Kong Repertory Theatre** (www.hkrep .com) and the more experimental **Chung Ying Theatre Company** (http:// www.chungying.com).

Honkywood!

Once considered a bastion of trashy violence, Hong Kong's film industry has caught the attention of Hollywood in recent years. Gravity-defying fight scenes and Bruce Lee-esque conflict resolution were once considered a cinematic joke, and in 1999 things were looking grim for Hong Kong cinema due only partly to the economic downturn and the boom in video piracy. But it all changed when Ang Lee's *Crouching Tiger, Hidden Dragon* won an Oscar for best foreign film in 2001. A small but productive independent film industry exists in Hong Kong, churning out around 150 films each year including international hits such as Wong Kar Wai's *In the Mood for Love* (2000) and the *Infernal Affairs* trilogy directed by Andrew Lau (Lau Wai Keung) and Alan Mak (Mak Siu Fai). The annual Hong Kong International Film Festival in April brings in more than 200 films worldwide and is now one of the world's major film festivals.

Directory

The serene sanctuary of Chi Lin Nunnery

ARRIVAL & DEPARTURE

Most international travellers arrive and depart via Hong Kong International Airport.

Travellers to and from mainland China can use ferry or rail links to Guangdong and beyond. It's also possible to fly or drive into Macau and catch a ferry from there.

Air

Hong Kong's sleek **Hong Kong International Airport** (1, E2; www .hkairport.com) is on an island flattened and extended by reclaimed land off the north coast of Lantau Island.

Highways, bridges (including the 2.2km-long Tsing Ma Bridge) and a fast train link the airport with Kowloon and Hong Kong Island.

INFORMATION

Airport General Inquiries ☎ 2181 0000; www.hkairport.com

Hotel Booking Service ☎ 2383 8300

Left Luggage ☎ 2261 0110

Air Canada ☎ 2867 8111

Air New Zealand ☎ 2862 8988

British Airways ☎ 2822 9000

Cathay Pacific ☎ 2747 1888

Qantas ☎ 2822 9000

United Airlines ☎ 2810 4888

AIRPORT ACCESS

Airport Express (☎ 2881 8888; www.mtr.com.hk) Trains depart from Hong Kong station ($100) in Central every 10 minutes from 5.50am to 12.48am daily, calling at Kowloon station ($90) in Jordan and at Tsing Yi Island ($60) en route. Vending machines dispense tickets at the airport and train stations en route. You can also use an Octopus card (p111). If you are booked on a scheduled flight and are taking the Airport Express, you can check in your bags and receive your boarding pass on the day of your flight at Hong Kong or Kowloon Airport Express station.

Buses A11 ($40) and A12 ($45) service major hotel and guesthouse areas on Hong Kong Island, and the A21 ($33) services similar areas in Kowloon. Buses run from about 6am to midnight; the 'N' buses follows the same route after midnight. Buy your ticket at the booth near the airport bus stand.

Taxis Airport to Central/Tsim Sha Tsui costs around $335/270.

Train

Getting to or from Shenzhen is a breeze. Just board the Kowloon-Canton Railway's East Rail (KCR; p112) at Hung Hom (3, F6) and ride it to Lo Wu ($33) on the mainland frontier.

The Kowloon–Guangzhou express train ($190, 1¾ hours) departs from the Hung Hom station about twelve times daily. Tickets can be booked in advance at KCR stations in Hung Hom, Mong Kok, Kowloon Tong and Sha Tin; from China Travel Service (CTS) agents; or over the phone (☎ 2947 7888).

Another rail line links Hung Hom with both Shanghai and Beijing. Trains to Beijing (hard/soft sleeper $574/934, 24 hours) via Guangzhou, Changsha and Wuhan, leave on alternate days. Trains to Shanghai ($508/825, 23 hours) via Guangzhou and Hangzhou also leave on alternate days.

Bus

Several transport companies in Hong Kong offer bus services to Guangzhou, the Shenzhen airport and other destinations in Guangdong. These include **Eternal East** (☎ 2723 2923; www.eebus.com),

CTS (☎ 2365 0118; http://ctsbus
.hkcts.com), the **Motor Transport
Company of Guangdong & Hong
Kong** (☎ 2317 7900; http://www
.gdhkmtc.com) and **Trans-Island
Limousine Service** (☎ 3193 9333;
www.trans-island.com.hk).

Boat
Services to and from Macau run
virtually around-the-clock. Boats
depart from the **Macau ferry terminal** (4, B1) in Sheung Wan,
and the **China ferry terminal** (3,
A7), Kowloon. Tickets ($142 from
Hong Kong Island, $140 from
Kowloon, higher prices at night
and weekends) can be bought at
the terminals or by calling ☎ 2859
3333 or ☎ 2131 8181.

Jet catamarans and hovercraft
leave both terminals (though primarily the China ferry terminal)
to destinations in neighbouring
Guangdong.

Travel Documents
PASSPORT
Must be valid for one month from
date of entry.

VISA
Visas are not required for citizens of the UK (up to 180 days),
citizens of other European Union
(EU) countries, Australia, Canada,
Japan, New Zealand and the USA
(90 days) and South Africa (30
days). Others should check visa
regulations (www.immd.gov.hk/eht
ml/hkvisas_4.htm) before leaving
home.

Customs & Duty Free
Firecrackers and fireworks are ban-
ned in Hong Kong but not in
Macau and mainland China, and
people crossing the border may
be searched for these. Customs
officers are on high alert for drug
smugglers. Meat, plant and textile
products are restricted.

The duty-free allowance for visitors is 200 cigarettes (or 50 cigars
or 250g tobacco) and 1L of alcohol
(wine or spirits).

Departure Tax
The Hong Kong airport departure
tax – $120 for everyone over 12
years – is always included in the
price of the ticket.

Left Luggage
There are left-luggage lockers in all
the major KCR train stations, the
Macau and China ferry terminals
and in the Hong Kong Airport
Express station.

You will also find a left-luggage
counter on Level 5 (Arrivals Hall)
of the Hong Kong International
Airport.

GETTING AROUND
Hong Kong is small and crowded,
and public transport is the only
practical way to move people.

The ultra-modern Mass Transit Railway (MTR) subway is the
quickest way to get to most urban
destinations.

The bus system is extensive and
as efficient as traffic allows, but it
can be bewildering for short-stay
travellers.

Ferries are fast and economical
and come with harbour views.

In this guide we include icons
that indicate the most practical
and convenient form of transport
for each listing.

Travel Passes
Octopus card (☎ 2266 2266; www
.octopuscards.com), a rechargeable
'smart card' valid on most forms
of public transport, costs $150.
This includes a $50 refundable
deposit and $100 worth of travel.

Octopus fares are between 5% and 10% cheaper than ordinary ones on the MTR and KCR.

For shorter stays there's the new **Tourist MTR 1-Day Pass** ($50), valid on the MTR for 24 hours.

Train
MASS TRANSIT RAILWAY (MTR)
The **MTR** (☎ 2881 8888; www.mtr .com.hk) is clean, fast and safe and transports around 2.5 million people daily. Tickets cost $4 to $26 ($3.80 to $23.10 with an Octopus card). Trains run every two to four minutes 6am to 1am daily on six lines (see inside front cover) including the Airport Express. Ticket machines accept $20 and $10 notes, as well as $10, $5, $2 and $1 and $0.50 coins, and also dispense change.

KOWLOON-CANTON RAILWAY (KCR)
Kowloon-Canton Railway (KCR; ☎ 2602 7799; www.kcrc.com) consists of two lines: KCR East Rail runs from Hung Hom station to Lo Wu on the mainland border, and the new KCR West Rail links Sham Shui Po in New Kowloon with Tuen Mun in the New Territories. The KCR is the fastest way to get up to the New Territories. The 30-minute ride to Sheung Shui/Tuen Mun costs $13/9, while the 40-minute trip to Lo Wu will set you back $33.

Bus
Hong Kong's extensive bus system will take you just about anywhere in the territory. Most buses run from 5.30am or 6am until midnight or 12.30am, though there are a handful of night buses that run from 12.45am to 5am. Bus fares are $1.20 to $45, depending on the destination, with night buses costing $12.80 to $23. You will need exact change or an Octopus card (see Travel Passes p111).

Central's most important bus terminal is below **Exchange Square** (4, C3). From here you can catch buses to Aberdeen, Repulse Bay, Stanley and other destinations on the southern side of Hong Kong Island. In Kowloon, the **Star Ferry bus terminal** (3, B9) has buses up Nathan Rd and to the Hung Hom station.

Figuring out which bus you want can be difficult although it's useful to know that any bus number ending with the letter M (eg 40) goes to an MTR station and that buses with an X are express.

PUBLIC LIGHT BUSES
Public 'light buses' (an official term that no one ever uses) are vans with no more than 16 seats. Small red 'minibuses' ($2.50 to $20) don't run regular routes; you can get on or off almost anywhere. Green 'maxicabs' operate on some 325 set routes and make designated stops. Two popular routes are the No 6 from Hankow Rd in Tsim Sha Tsui to Tsim Sha Tsui East and Hung Hom station in Kowloon, and the No 1 to Victoria Peak from east of the Star Ferry pier in Central.

Tram
Hong Kong Island's double-decker trams (p15) are not fast but are fun and cheap. For a flat fare of $2 (dropped in a box beside the driver when you leave) you can rattle along as far as you like over 16km of track. Trams operate 6am to 1am, and run every two to 10 minutes. Try to get a seat at the front window upstairs to enjoy a first-class view.

Hong Kong has six tram routes: Kennedy Town–Western Market, Kennedy Town–Happy

Valley–Causeway Bay, Sai Ying Pun (Whitty St)–North Point, Happy Valley–Shau Kei Wan and Sheung Wan (Western Market)–Shau Kei Wan.

Strictly speaking a funicular, the **Peak Tram** (one-way/return adult $20/30, child 3-11 years $6/9, senior $7/14) departs for Victoria Peak about every 10 to 15 minutes from 7am to midnight. The tram's **lower terminus** (4, D4) is behind St John's Building at 33 Garden Rd, Central at the northwestern corner of Hong Kong Park, some 650m from the Star Ferry pier. See p10 for more details.

Boat

There are four Star Ferry (p9) routes, but by far the most popular is the one running between **Central** (4, D3) and **Tsim Sha Tsui** (3, B9). The trip takes seven minutes and fares are $1.70/2.20 (lower/upper deck). Star Ferries also link Central with Hung Hom and Wan Chai with Hung Hom and Tsim Sha Tsui.

Three other ferry companies operate cross-harbour routes but the only one of interest to travellers is the hydrofoil from **Queen's Pier** (4, D3) in Central to Tsim Sha Tsui East. Two separate ferry companies operate services to the outlying islands, including Lantau, Cheung Chau, Peng Chau and Lamma, from **piers 4, 5 and 6** (4, D2) in Central.

Taxi

Hong Kong taxis are a bargain in comparison with cabs in other big cities. The flag fall for taxis on Hong Kong Island and Kowloon is $15 for the first 2km and $1.40 for every additional 200m. It's slightly less in the New Territories and on Lantau Island.

Car & Motorcycle

No matter how long your visit to Hong Kong, it is highly unlikely that you'll need your own wheels. The traffic often slows to a crawl here, and finding a parking space is difficult and very expensive.

If you do need to hire a vehicle, try **Ace Hire Car** (☎ 2572 7663, 2893 0541; www.acehirecar.com .hk), which has chauffeur-driven cars for $160 to $250 per hour (minimum two to five hours).

If you're hell-bent on driving yourself (crazy), **Avis** (5, B4; ☎ 2890 6988; fax 2895 0371; Ground fl, Bright Star Mansion, 93 Leighton Rd, Causeway Bay) charges $720/3200 for a day/week with unlimited kilometres.

PRACTICALITIES
Business Hours

Business hours are Monday to Friday 9am to 5.30pm or 6pm, and Saturday 9am to noon or 1pm. Many offices close for lunch between 1pm and 2pm.

Stores catering to the tourist trade keep longer hours, but almost nothing opens before 9am, and many stores don't open until 10am or 10.30am. Even tourist-related businesses shut down by 10pm.

Most banks, post offices, shops and attractions are closed on public holidays; restaurants usually open daily, including Sunday.

Climate & When to Go

October, November and nearly all of December are the best months to visit Hong Kong. Temperatures at these times are moderate, the skies are clear and the sun shines. January and February are cloudy and cold but dry. It's warmer from March to May but humid, with lots of fog and drizzle. From June to September the sweltering heat and humidity can make for some sweaty sightseeing.

Travel in and out of Hong Kong can be difficult during Chinese New Year, which falls in late January or early February.

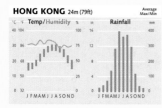

Consulates

Hong Kong is one of the world's most consulate-clogged cities.

Australia (7, C2; ☎ 2827 8881; 23rd fl, Harbour Centre, 25 Harbour Rd, Wan Chai)

Canada (4, C3; ☎ 2810 4321; 11th-14th fl, Tower I, Exchange Sq, 8 Connaught Pl, Central)

New Zealand (7, B2; ☎ 2877 4488; Rm 6508, 65th fl, Central Plaza, 18 Harbour Rd, Wan Chai)

South Africa (7, C2; ☎ 2577 3279; Rm 2706-2710, 27th fl, Great Eagle Centre, 23 Harbour Rd, Wan Chai)

UK (4, E5; ☎ 2901 3000; 1 Supreme Court Rd, Admiralty)

USA (4, D4; ☎ 2523 9011; 26 Garden Rd, Central)

Disabled Travellers

Disabled people will have to cope with MTR and KCR stairs as well as pedestrian overpasses, narrow footpaths and steep hills. People whose sight or hearing is impaired must be cautious of Hong Kong's demon drivers. On the other hand, some buses are now accessible by wheelchair, taxis are never hard to find and most buildings have lifts (many with Braille panels). Wheelchairs can negotiate the lower decks of most of the ferries, and almost all public toilets now have access for the disabled.

Contact the **Joint Council for the Physically and Mentally Disabled** (7, A3; ☎ 2864 2929; fax 2865 4916; Rm 1204, 12th fl, Duke of Windsor Social Service Bldg, 15 Hennessy Rd, Wan Chai).

Discounts

Children and seniors are generally offered half-price at attractions and on most forms of transport, but family tickets are rare. The Hong Kong Museums Pass (p27) is worth considering.

STUDENT & YOUTH CARDS

The International Student Identity Card (ISIC) offers discounts on some forms of transport and cheaper admission to museums and other attractions. If you're under 26 but not a student, you can apply for an International Youth Travel Card (IYTC) card issued by the Federation of International Youth Travel Organisations (FIYTO), which gives much the same discounts.

Electricity

The standard voltage is 220V, 50Hz AC. The shape of pins and prongs on plugs can vary, but inexpensive adaptors are widely available.

Emergencies

Hong Kong is generally very safe both night and day but, as with anywhere, things can go wrong.

Ambulance, Fire & Police ☎ 999
Police (non-emergency) ☎ 2527 7177
Rape Crisis Line ☎ 2375 5322

Fitness

Walking and *taijiquan* (or t'ai chi) are the most popular physical activities in Hong Kong. Golf is generally a rich person's sport, undertaken more for networking and prestige than fitness. Tennis and gym sessions are also popular, and most top-end hotels have gyms and pools. Both Kowloon Park (p33) and Victoria Park (p10) have swimming pools that are more for leisure than laps.

Several fitness clubs in Hong Kong allow short-term memberships for $150 to $200 per day, including:

California Fitness (6, C3; ☎ 2522 5229; www.californiafitness.com; 1 Wellington St, Central) There are some six outlets in Hong Kong.

Pure Fitness (6, A2; ☎ 2970 3366; www.pure-fit.com; 1st-3rd fl, Kinwick Centre, 32 Hollywood Rd, Central) Enter this favourite of the Soho set from Shelley St.

Gay & Lesbian Travellers

Despite the removal in 1991 of criminal penalties for homosexual acts between those over 18 years old, people remain relatively conservative about homosexuality.

Horizons (☎ 2815 9268; www .horizons.org.hk) is an advice and counselling service for gays, lesbians and bisexuals. See also p92 for details on gay and lesbian entertainment listings.

Health
DENTAL SERVICES

Private dental clinics can be found throughout Hong Kong; some hospitals offer emergency dental services. To find a dentist, ask your hotel or contact the **Dental Council** (☎ 2873 5862; www.dchk.org.hk).

IMMUNISATIONS & PRECAUTIONS

There are no specific vaccination requirements for Hong Kong or Macau.

The Severe Acute Respiratory Syndrome (SARS) 'epidemic' notwithstanding (see p102), health conditions in Hong Kong are good. The government insists that Hong Kong's tap water is perfectly safe to drink but bottled water is widely available for the wary.

Take the usual precautions when it comes to sex; condoms are available in pharmacies, supermarkets and convenience stores.

MEDICAL SERVICES

Travel insurance is advisable to cover any medical treatment you may need while in Hong Kong. Medical care is generally of a high standard, though public hospital facilities are stretched and private hospital treatment fairly expensive.

The hospital general inquiry number is ☎ 2300 6555. The following hospitals have 24-hour accident and emergency departments:

Hong Kong Central Hospital (6, C3; ☎ 2537 8441; 1b Lower Albert Rd, Central) Private hospital.

Hong Kong Medical Association (HKMA; ☎ 90000 223 322) MediLink hotline with recorded information.

Matilda International Hospital (2, A2; ☎ 2849 0700, 24hr hotline ☎ 2849 0111; 41 Mt Kellett Rd, Peak) Private hospital.

Queen Elizabeth Hospital (3, D4; ☎ 2958 8888; 30 Gascoigne Rd, Yau Ma Tei) Public hospital.

PHARMACIES

Watson's the Chemist and **Mannings** are pharmacy chains with branches across Hong Kong; most are open until 10pm. The hospitals listed earlier have dispensing chemists on duty 24 hours.

TRADITIONAL MEDICINE

Traditional Chinese medicine is extremely popular in Hong Kong, both as a preventative and a cure. See p62 for more information.

Holidays

1 Jan	New Year's Day
Late Jan/Feb	Chinese New Year (3 days)
Late Mar/Apr	Easter (3 days)
Early Apr	Ching Ming
Late Apr/May	Buddha's Birthday
1 May	Labour Day
June	Dragon Boat Festival
1 July	Hong Kong SAR Establishment Day
Sep/Oct	Mid-Autumn Festival
1 & 2 Oct	China National Day
Oct	Cheung Yeung
25 Dec	Christmas Day
26 Dec	Boxing Day

Internet
INTERNET SERVICE PROVIDERS
Local ISPs include PCCW's **Netvigator** (☎ 1833 833; www.netvigator.com) and **HKNet** (☎ 2110 2288; www.hknet.com). America On-line's customer service number is ☎ 2250 5678; Yahoo's customer service number is ☎ 2895 5769.

INTERNET CAFÉS
If you can't access the Internet from your hotel, Hong Kong has plenty of independent options:
Central Library (5, C4; ☎ 2921 0503; www.hkpl.gov.hk; 66 Causeway Rd, Causeway Bay) Free access.
Cyber Clan (3, C8; ☎ 2523 2821; South Basement, Golden Crown Ct, 66-70 Nathan Rd, Tsim Sha Tsui)
IT.fans (6, B1; ☎ 2542 1868; Ground fl, Man On Commercial Bldg, 12-13 Jubilee St, Central)
Pacific Coffee Company (4, D2; ☎ 2868 5100; www.pacificcoffee.com; Shop 1022, 1st fl, IFC Mall, 1 Harbour View St, Central) Located in the IFC Mall; free access with purchase.

USEFUL WEBSITES
The Lonely Planet Website (www.lonelyplanet.com) is a good start for many of Hong Kong's more useful links. Other handy websites include:
Hong Kong Information
  www.info.gov.hk
Hong Kong Telephone Directory
www.pccw.com
Hong Kong Tourism Board
  www.discoverhongkong.com
Hong Kong Weather
  www.weather.org.hk
South China Morning Post
  www.scmp.com.hk

Lost Property
Each public transport service manages its own lost property:
Citybus (☎ 2873 0818; www.citybus.com.hk)
Hong Kong & Kowloon Ferry (☎ 2815 6063; www.hkkf.com.hk)
Hongkong Tramways (☎ 2548 7102; www.info.gov.hk/td/eng/transport/tram.html)
KCR (☎ 2602 7799; www.kcrc.com)
Kowloon Motor Bus Co (☎ 2745 4466; www.kmb.com.hk)
MTR (☎ 2861 0020; www.mtr.com.hk)
New World First Bus Services (☎ 2136 8888; www.nwfb.com.hk)
New World First Ferry (☎ 2131 8181; www.nwff.com.hk)
Peak Tram (☎ 2849 7654; www.thepeak.com.hk)
Star Ferry (☎ 2366 2576; www.starferry.com.hk)

Metric System
Although the international metric system is in official use, traditional Chinese weights and measures are still common. At local markets, items are sold by the *leung* (37.8g)

and the *gan* (catty; about 605g). There are 16 *leung* to the *gan*.

Money

ATMS

International travellers can withdraw funds from their home accounts using just about any of the numerous ATMs scattered around town. Few, if any, charge a fee for the service.

CREDIT CARDS

The most widely accepted credit cards in Hong Kong are Visa, MasterCard, American Express, Diners Club and JCB. For 24-hour card cancellations or assistance, try calling the following numbers:

American Express	☎ 2811 6122
Diners Club	☎ 2860 1888
JCB	☎ 2366 7211
MasterCard	☎ 2598 8038
Visa	☎ 2810 8033

CURRENCY

The local currency is the Hong Kong dollar ($ throughout this book). The dollar is divided into 100c. Notes are issued in denominations of $10, $20, $50, $100, $500 and $1000. There are coins of 10c, 20c, 50c, $1, $2, $5 and $10.

MONEYCHANGERS

Licensed moneychangers such as Chequepoint abound in tourist areas and keep extensive hours. There is no commission, but the exchange rates offered are equivalent to a 5% commission. Banks have marginally better rates.

TRAVELLERS CHEQUES

Most banks cash travellers cheques for a fee of $50 to $100. Licensed moneychangers don't levy a commission but often give a lower rate of exchange.

Newspapers & Magazines

The local English-language newspapers are the *South China Morning Post* ($7), published daily, and the *Hong Kong Standard* ($6), published Monday to Friday and once at the weekend. Asian editions of the *International Herald Tribune,* the *Financial Times,* the *Asian Wall Street Journal* and *USA Today* are printed in Hong Kong.

Photography

Any photographic accessory you could possibly need is available in Hong Kong. **Stanley St** (4, C3) on Hong Kong Island is the place to look for reputable camera stores.

Post

On Hong Kong Island, the **General Post Office** (GPO; 4, D3; 2 Connaught Pl, Central) is just west of the Star Ferry. There's also a **Kowloon post office** (3, C8; 10 Middle Rd) in Tsim Sha Tsui. Both are open 8am to 6pm Monday to Saturday, and 9am to 2pm Sunday. You'll find stamp vending machines outside most post offices. The postal services inquiry number is ☎ 2921 2222.

Allow five days for delivery of letters, postcards and aerogrammes to the UK, USA and Australia. **Speedpost** (☎ 2921 2277) reduces delivery time by half.

Airmail letters and postcards are $2.40 (to Asia except Japan) and $3 (elsewhere) for the first 20g and $1.20 and $1.30 respectively for each additional 10g. Aerogrammes are $2.30 for both zones.

Radio

Popular English-language radio stations in Hong Kong are RTHK

Radio 3 (current affairs and talk-back; 567AM, 1584AM, 97.9FM and 106.8FM), RTHK Radio 4 (classical music; 97.6FM to 98.9FM), RTHK Radio 6 (BBC World Service relays; 675AM); HMV Radio (hit parade; 864AM); and Metro Plus (news; 1044AM).

The *South China Morning Post* publishes a daily guide to radio programs.

Telephone

All calls made within Hong Kong are local calls and therefore free, except at public payphones, where they cost $1 for five minutes.

PHONECARDS

International direct-dial (IDD) calls can be made to almost anywhere in the world from public phones, but you'll need a phonecard. These are available as stored-value cards ($100), which allow you to call from any phone – public or private – by punching in a PIN code, and as Hello Smartcards (five denominations, $50 to $500), which work in payphones. You can buy them at 7-Eleven and Circle K convenience stores, Mannings pharmacies and Wellcome supermarkets.

MOBILE PHONES

Hong Kong boasts the world's highest per-capita usage of mobile telephones and pagers and they work everywhere – even in tunnels and the MTR. Any GSM-compatible phone can be used in Hong Kong.

PCCW shops rent and sell mobile phones, SIM cards and phone accessories. Handsets can be rented for $35 per day, and rechargeable SIM chips cost HK$180/280 for 360/560 minutes. The SIM chips and phones are IDD compatible,

but there's an extra charge if you need a roaming service to take to Macau or mainland China.

COUNTRY CODES

Australia	☎ 61
Canada	☎ 1
China (Mainland)	☎ 86
Hong Kong	☎ 852
Japan	☎ 81
Macau	☎ 853
New Zealand	☎ 64
South Africa	☎ 27
UK	☎ 44
USA	☎ 1

USEFUL PHONE NUMBERS

Local Directory Inquiries	☎ 1081
International Directory Inquiries	☎ 10013
International Access Code	☎ 001
International Fax Dialling Code	☎ 002
Reverse-Charge (collect)	☎ 10010
International Credit Card	☎ 10011
Time & Air Temperature	☎ 18501

Television

The two English-language stations are TVB Pearl and ATV World. The program schedule is listed daily in the *South China Morning Post* and in a weekly Sunday supplement.

Time

Hong Kong Standard Time is eight hours ahead of GMT; summer/daylight-savings time isn't practised.

Tipping

In general, tipping is not done in Hong Kong; taxi drivers only expect you to round up to the nearest dollar. Tip hotel porters at least $10 and, if you make use of airport porters, $2 a suitcase is normally expected. However, most upmarket restaurants and hotels add a 10% service charge to their bills.

Toilets

Hong Kong has never had as many public toilets as other world-class cities, but that is changing rapidly, with some new ones being built and old ones reopened. The toilets are always free and almost all now have disabled access and baby-changing shelves in both men's and women's rooms. Equip yourself with tissues, though; public toilets in Hong Kong are often out of toilet paper.

Tourist Information

The very efficient and friendly **Hong Kong Tourism Board** (HKTB; www.discoverhongkong .com) produces reams of useful pamphlets and publications. Its website is also a good point of reference.

There are HKTB branches at **Hong Kong International Airport** (1, B2), **Star Ferry Concourse** (3, B9) in Tsim Sha Tsui, and on the ground floor of the **Center** (4, C2) in Central. Alternatively, call the **HKTB Visitor Hotline** (☎ 2508 1234; ☷ 8am-6pm).

Women Travellers

Few women visitors or residents complain of bad treatment, intimidation or aggression, and for the most part a Hong Kong experience should be hassle-free. Having said that, some Chinese men look upon Western women as 'easy' and have made passes at foreigners, even in public places.

Tampons are widely available, but there's not a lot of variety as most Hong Kong women prefer sanitary pads. The contraceptive pill is available by prescription only.

LANGUAGE

Cantonese and English are Hong Kong's two official languages. While Cantonese is used in Hong Kong in everyday life by most (some 94%) of the population, English is still the primary language of commerce, banking, international trade and the higher courts.

However, there has been a dramatic rise in the number of Mandarin-speaking tourists since the handover, and some locals are now learning Mandarin in preference to English. Still, short-term English-speaking visitors can get along fine in much of Hong Kong without a word of Cantonese; street signs and public transport information are presented in both English and Chinese, for example.

Of course, in the back streets, markets and non-touristy restaurants, communicating with local people will be more difficult.

TONES & ROMANISATION

Chinese languages have many homonyms (words that sound alike). What distinguishes the meaning of these words are the changes in a speaker's pitch or tone and the context of the word within the sentence.

Explaining the tonal system and the Romanisation systems used to render Chinese characters into a form Westerners can read and pronounce is beyond the scope of this book. Therefore, the words and phrases we've included here use a simplified system of Romanisation and are not marked for tones.

For an in-depth guide to the language, get a copy of Lonely Planet's *Cantonese phrasebook*.

PRONOUNS

I/me	*ngoh*
you	*nei*
he/she/it	*kui*
we/us	*ngoh dei*
you (pl)	*nei dei*
they/them	*kui dei*

BASICS

Hello, how are you?	*nei ho?*
I'm fine.	*ngoh gei ho.*
Good morning.	*jo san.*
Goodbye.	*baai baai.*
Goodnight.	*jo tau.*
Excuse me.	*m goi.*
I'm sorry.	*dui m jue.*
Thanks	*do je.*
(for a gift or favour)	
You're welcome.	*m sai haak hei.*

SMALL TALK

What is your surname?
  cheng man gwai sing?
My surname is ...
  siu sing ...
My name is ...
  ngoh giu ...
This is Mr/Mrs/Ms (Lee)
  ni wai hai (lei) sin saang/
  taai taai/siu je
Glad to meet you.
  ho go hing ying sik nei
Can you please help me take a photo?
  ho m ho yi bong ngoh ying jeung
  seung a?
Is it OK to take a photo?
  ho m ho yi ying seung a?

LANGUAGE DIFFICULTIES

Do you speak English?
  nei sik m sik gong ying man a?

Do you understand?
  nei ming m ming a?
I understand.
  ngoh ming.
I don't understand.
  ngoh m ming.
Can you repeat that please?
  cheng joi gong yat chi?
What is this called?
  ni goh giu mat ye a?

GETTING AROUND

Go straight ahead.	*yat jik hui.*
left/right	*joh bin/yau bin*
airport	*gei cheung*
bus stop	*ba si jaam*
ferry pier	*siu lin ma tau*
subway station	*dei tit jaam*
information centre	*sun man chue*
north	*bak*
south	*naam*
east	*dung*
west	*sai*

I'd like to go to ...
  ngoh seung hui ...
Does this (bus) go to ...?
  ni ga (ba si) hui m hui ... a?
How much is the fare?
  gei doh chin a?
I want to get off at ...
  ngoh seung hai ... lok che
Stop here please.
  m goi, ni do/yau lok (taxi/minibus).
Where is the ... please?
  cheng man ... hai bin do a?
Is it far?
  yuen m yuen a?
Please write down the address for me.
  m goi se goh dei ji bei ngoh.

ACCOMMODATION

Do you have any rooms?
yau mo fong a?
I'd like a (single/double) room.
ngoh seung yiu yat goh (daan/seung)
yan fong.
I'd like a quiet room.
ngoh seung yiu yat gaan
jing di gefong
How much per night?
gei doh chin yat maan a?

EATING & DRINKING

restaurant	*chaan teng*
bar	*jau ba*
food court/street	*sik gaai*
delicious	*ho ho me*

I'm a vegetarian.
ngoh hai so sik ge.
Do you have an English menu?
yau mo ying man chaan paai a?
Can you recommend any dishes?
yau mat ye ho gaai siu a?
I'd like the set menu, please.
ngoh yiu goh to chaan.
Please bring me (a knife and fork).
m goi loh (yat foo do cha)
bei ngoh.
Please bring the bill.
m goi maai daan.

SHOPPING

How much is this?
ni goh gei doh chin a?
That's very expensive.
ho gwai.
Can you reduce the price?
peng di dak m dak a?
I'm just looking.
ngoh sin tai yat tai.

HEALTH

I'm sick.
ngoh yau beng.
My friend is sick.
ngoh pang yau yau beng.
I need a doctor.
ngoh yiu tai yi sang.
It hurts here.
ni do m sue fuk.
I have asthma.
ngoh haau chuen.
I have diarrhoea.
ngoh to ngoh.
I'd like to see a female doctor
dorngoh yiu wan yat wai nui yi sang.
I'm allergic to (antibiotics/penicillin).
ngoh dui (kong sang so/
poon nei sai lam) gwoh man.

EMERGENCIES

Help!
gau meng a!
Thief!
cheung ye a!
Call the police!
giu ging chaat!
Call an ambulance!
giu gau seung che!
Watch out!
siu sam!

DAYS & NUMBERS

day	*yat*
week	*sing kei*
today	*gam yat*
tomorrow	*ting yat*
yesterday	*kam yat*
0	*ling*
1	*yat*
2	*yi* (or *leung*
	with noun)

3	*saam*	10	*sap*
4	*sei*	11	*sap yat*
5	*ng*	12	*sap yi*
6	*luk*	20	*yi sap*
7	*chat*	21	*yi sap yat*
8	*baat*	100	*yat baak*
9	*gau*	1000	*yat chin*

Index

SHOPPING

EATING

SLEEPING

Sights – Quick Index

FEATURES

- 🏯 Korea Garden.....................*Eating*
- 🎦 JP Cinema....................*Entertainment*
- 🍷 Rice Bar..............................*Drinking*
- 🏛 Hong Kong Museum...........*Highlights*
- 🛍 King Fook..............................*Shopping*
- 🏛 KS Lo Gallery............*Sights/Activities*
- 🏠 Excelsior Hong Kong.............*Sleeping*

AREAS

- ....Beach, Desert
- ....Building
- ....Land
- ....Mall
- ....Other Area
- ....Park/Cemetery
- ....Sports
- ....Urban

HYDROGRAPHY

- ....River, Creek
- ....Intermittent River
- ....Canal
- ....Swamp
- ....Water

BOUNDARIES

- ....State, Provincial
- ....Regional, Suburb
- ....Ancient Wall

ROUTES

- ....Tollway
- ....Freeway
- ....Primary Road
- ....Secondary Road
- ....Tertiary Road
- ....Lane
- ....Under Construction
- ....One-Way Street
- ....Unsealed Road
- ....Mall/Steps
- ....Tunnel
- ....Walking Path
- ....Walking Trail/Track
- ....Pedestrian Overpass
- ....Walking Tour

TRANSPORT

- ....Airport, Airfield
- ....Bus Route
- ....Cycling, Bicycle Path
- ....Ferry
- ....General Transport
- ....Metro
- ....Rail
- ....Taxi Rank
- ....Tram

SYMBOLS

- ....Bank, ATM
- ....Buddhist
- ....Castle, Fortress
- ....Christian
- ....Diving, Snorkeling
- ....Embassy, Consulate
- ....Hospital, Clinic
- ....Information
- ....Internet Access
- ....Islamic
- ....Jewish
- ....Lighthouse
- ....Lookout
- ....Monument
- ....Mountain, Volcano
- ....National Park
- ....Parking Area
- ....Petrol Station
- ....Picnic Area
- ....Point of Interest
- ....Police Station
- ....Post Office
- ....Telephone
- ....Toilets
- ....Zoo, Bird Sanctuary
- ....Waterfall

24/7 travel advice
www.lonelyplanet.com